Unterrichtsmodell

Series Editor: Hans Kröger

T. C. Boyle

The Tortilla Curtain

by Wiltrud Frenken,
Angela Luz and
Brigitte Prischtt

Schöningh

EINFACH ENGLISCH

- Arbeitsfrage
- filmische Präsentation
- Einzelarbeit
- Partnerarbeit
- Gruppenarbeit
- Unterrichtsgespräch
- Schreibauftrag
- Hausaufgabe
- Projektorientierung, offenes Unterrichtsangebot
- Aufgaben mit kreativem Ansatz
- Szenisches Spiel, Rollenspiel

Vorwort

Der Titel der Reihe **EinFach Englisch** ist Ziel und Programm zugleich. Einerseits sollen Schülerinnen und Schülern literarische Zusammenhänge erklärt und ihnen damit der Zugang zu klassischen, aber auch neueren literarischen Werken erleichtert werden, und dies soll auf sprachlich einfache Art und Weise erfolgen, wodurch man der heutigen Schülergeneration sicherlich eher gerecht werden kann als mit schwierigen und komplexen Ansätzen. Andererseits sollen Lehrkräften erprobte und aus der Praxis stammende Unterrichtsmodelle angeboten werden, die ihnen einen raschen Zugriff auf unterschiedliche Materialien ermöglichen und einen Leitfaden für die Behandlung fiktionaler Texte oder die Analyse von Filmen im Unterricht bieten. Die Modelle können direkt und ohne Umschweife eingesetzt werden, langes Einlesen und eine zeitintensive Beschäftigung mit dem Stoff sind nicht erforderlich, wodurch die Arbeit, insbesondere die Unterrichtsvorbereitung von Lehrerinnen und Lehrern, erheblich erleichtert werden kann.
Schnell erhält man einen Überblick über **Figurenkonstellation** und **Inhalt** und kann sich problemlos entscheiden, ob ein Werk für eine bestimmte Reihe geeignet ist. Man weiß vorab, welche **Klausur** mit welchen Schwerpunkten geschrieben werden kann, und kann dieses bei der konkreten Planung eines Kursabschnittes entsprechend berücksichtigen. **Arbeitsblätter** sind als Kopiervorlagen gestaltet und **Tafelbilder** sind eingebettet in die **Leitfragen** zum eigentlichen Unterrichtsgeschehen, d. h., Material, das eingesetzt werden soll, befindet sich dort, wo es gebraucht wird; langes Suchen entfällt. **Piktogramme** geben optische Hilfen und Hinweise, sodass leicht zu erkennen ist, welche **Sozial-** bzw. **Arbeitsformen** sich bei den jeweiligen Aufgaben anbieten.
Die Unterrichtsmodelle basieren auf bewährten Verfahren der Textinterpretation und der Filmanalyse, dabei fließen neuere Erkenntnisse und Ansätze zu einer modernen Textrezeption angemessen ein. Der Umfang des Materials ist auf die tatsächlichen Gegebenheiten der Unterrichtspraxis abgestimmt und es sollte möglich sein, das Unterrichtsmodell vollständig und nicht nur in Auszügen im Rahmen einer Unterrichtsreihe einzusetzen. Das Prinzip der **„Components“** ermöglicht es darüber hinaus den Benutzern, unterschiedliche Reihen zu konzipieren, die an unterschiedlichen thematischen Schwerpunkten oder methodischen Fertigkeiten orientiert sind und ganz den individuellen oder kursspezifischen Bedürfnissen angepasst werden können. Dabei erheben die Unterrichtsmodelle nicht den Anspruch der Vollständigkeit, sondern eher den der Machbarkeit und Praxisnähe.

Sprachliche Betreuung: Geoffrey Perrin

www.schoeningh-schulbuch.de
Schöningh Verlag, Jühenplatz 1–3, 33098 Paderborn

Druck A 7 6 5 / Jahr 2009 08 07
Alle Drucke der Serie A sind im Unterricht parallel verwendbar.
Die letzte Zahl bezeichnet das Jahr dieses Druckes.

Umschlaggestaltung: Peter und Veronika Wypior
Druck und Bindung: Friedric Pustet, Regensburg

ISBN 978-3-14-041203-2

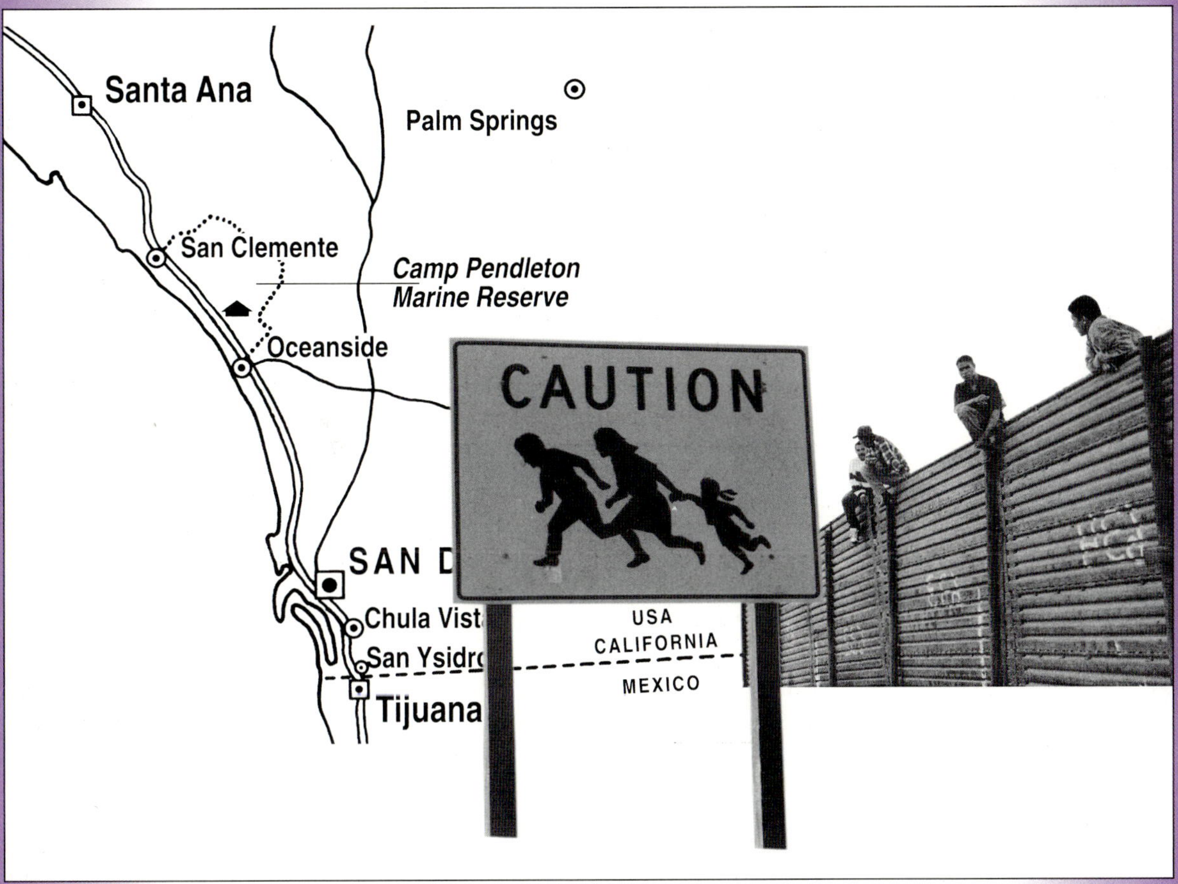

Collage: Víctor Prischtt

Components

T. C. Boyle: The Tortilla Curtain

Component 1
When Worlds Clash (Part One, pp. 3-142)

1.1 First encounter and clashes between the two worlds	I.1, I.6	text/board/discussion worksheets 1 and 2
1.2 Conflicting points of view towards the immigration issue	I.3, I.7	text/board/discussion worksheets 3 and 4

Component 2
Cándido's and América's Best of All Worlds (Part One, pp. 3-142)

2.1 Symbolism	I.4	text/board/discussion worksheet 5
2.2 América – everybody's victim	I.2, I.6, I.8	text/board

Component 3
When Mexican Dreams Meet US Reality (Part Two, pp. 145-257)

3.1 Delaney's worries	II.1, II.2, II.3	text/board/discussion worksheet 6
3.2 When Whites and Mexicans meet	II.1, II.2, II.3	text/board/discussion
3.3 The Mexicans' desperate struggle for happiness	II.2, II.4, II.7	text/board/discussion

Component 4
Delaney – Racist in a Liberal Skin (Parts One, Two and Three)

4.1 The wound refusing to heal	I.1, I.7, II.1	text/board/discussion worksheet 7
4.2 The long way to racism	II.1, II.3, II.5, II.6, III.3, III.6–8	text/board/discussion worksheet 8

Contents

Die Personen

DELANEY MOSSBACHER	Delaney lebt mit seiner zweiten Frau Kyra und seinem sechsjährigen Stiefsohn Jordan in dem neu erschlossenen Wohngebiet Arroyo Blanco weit ab vom Stadtkern von Los Angeles. Er ist als freischaffender Schriftsteller für ein Naturmagazin tätig. Delaney bezeichnet sich zunächst als liberal, was sich jedoch im Verlauf des Romans ändert.
KYRA MOSSBACHER	Kyra ist eine sehr erfolgreiche Immobilienmaklerin, die für den Unterhalt der Familie aufkommt. Sie betrachtet die Einwanderer aus Mexiko als Bedrohung für ihre Geschäfte.
CÁNDIDO	Der illegal eingewanderte Mexikaner Cándido (Mitte 30) lebt mit seiner Freundin América in einem Canyon in der Nähe von Arroyo Blanco. Er hat bereits mehrfach illegal in den USA gearbeitet und den Verdienst seiner Ex-Frau nach Mexiko gebracht; diesmal ist sein Ziel, genug Geld zu verdienen, um sich mit América ein Apartment leisten zu können und in den USA zu bleiben.
AMÉRICA	América ist 17 Jahre alt, schwanger und voller Illusionen mit Cándido in die USA gekommen, um dort ein neues Leben in einem kleinen Häuschen mit bescheidenem Wohlstand zu beginnen.
JACK JARDINE	Jack ist Anwalt und ein Wortführer in Arroyo Blanco. Er fordert vehement verschärfte Sicherheitsmaßnahmen bis hin zu einer Mauer rund um die Anlage. Er hält alle Einwanderer für eine Bedrohung seines Lebensstandards. Seine politische Haltung ist äußerst reaktionär.
JOSÉ NAVIDAD	José verkörpert die Bedrohung, die die Weißen in den Mexikanern sehen. Er vergewaltigt América, stiehlt ihr Geld und wendet sich so auch gegen seine eigenen Landsleute.

Der Inhalt

Der Roman *The Tortilla Curtain* (auf deutsch unter dem Titel *América* erschienen) spielt in einem der vielen Vororte von Los Angeles, in die sich die weißen Bewohner dieser Metropole auf der Flucht vor Verbrechen und Einwanderern und auf der Suche nach Natur zurückziehen. Der Leser trifft zwei Familien, die weißen Mossbachers, die mit ihrem Sohn in einer der neu erstellten Siedlungen für gut verdienende weiße Mittelständler leben, und die illegalen mexikanischen Einwanderer Cándido und América, die ihr erstes Kind erwarten und unter freiem Himmel kampieren.

Die Handlung setzt damit ein, dass Delaney auf einer Schnellstraße Cándido anfährt und ihn dabei verletzt. Er zahlt dem verschreckten Mexikaner 20 Dollar. Von nun an wechselt mit jedem Kapitel die Perspektive, der Leser verfolgt sowohl das Leben der Weißen wie auch das Leben der Mexikaner. Beiden Paaren widerfahren zunehmend schrecklichere Dinge. Delaneys Auto wird gestohlen, beide Hunde der Familie werden von Koyoten gerissen, Kyra wird bedroht, ihr Heim wird fast von einem Feuersturm zerstört. Durch diese Ereignisse und die Gespräche mit seiner Frau und seinen Freunden und Nachbarn wird Delaney immer mehr zum Reaktionär, obwohl er sich zu Beginn des Romans selbst als liberal bezeichnet.

Die ohnehin schon unerträglichen Lebensbedingungen der Mexikaner verschlechtern sich ebenfalls ständig. Cándido leidet unter den Folgen des Autounfalls, América wird vergewaltigt, Cándido wird von einem Landsmann überfallen, sie verlieren in dem Feuersturm alle ihre Ersparnisse, ihr Baby wird blind geboren. Am Ende des Romans reißt eine riesige Schlammflut alles in die Tiefe.

Part One

1	Delaney Cándido Kenny Grissom	– Delaney hits Cándido with his car and injures him – pays him 20 dollars – takes car to dealer
2	Cándido América	– Cándido runs a high fever but recovers, has feverish dreams about Mexico – América decides to go to the labour exchange
3	Delaney Kyra Jack Jardine	– one of the Mossbachers' dogs is savaged by a coyote in their back yard – During one of the community's meetings Delaney tries to convince his neighbours of dangers of feeding wildlife – community is preoccupied with discussion about gate for estate
4	Cándido América	– Cándido remembers his relationship with his wife Resurrección, América's older sister – América tries to find work in vain – two young men, possibly Jack Jardine's son and a friend, smash up Cándido's and América's camp in the canyon
5	Delaney Kyra	– Kyra shows her favourite house, the Da Ros place, to a couple – Delaney's column about wilderness at night

6	Cándido América	– América is offered a cup of coffee by a fellow Mexican at the labour exchange – she finds a job scrubbing buddhas for a fat white man at Arroyo Blanco – Cándido also meets intrusive Mexican when looking for América
7	Delaney Jack Jardine Cándido	– Delaney discusses illegals with Jack, they see Cándido at the supermarket's parking lot – Delaney decides to go for a hike, he also meets the unpleasant Mexican on the trail – returning to his car he finds it stolen
8	Cándido América	– América and Cándido buy food from her money, she can work again the next day – When she comes back from work Cándido is not there so she sets out on her own. On the way she is mugged and raped by the intrusive Mexican and his friend.

Part Two

1	Delaney K. Grissom Kyra	– Delaney buys new car – Delaney wants to go for a hike and ends up cowering behind the bushes and watching his new car – closing down the Da Ros place Kyra is threatened by the two Mexicans who have raped América
2	Cándido América	– Cándido finds a job putting up the Mossbachers' fence, – he remembers other times when he was working in the USA – when returning América tells him that her money has been stolen
3	Delaney Kyra D. Flood	– meeting at D. Flood's house (he is under arrest) – members of community discuss being walled in for protection – another coyote breaks into backyard and takes other dog
4	Cándido América	– labour exchange is closed so Cándido and América set out to Canoga Park where they learn that there are no jobs – a man offers help, Cándido leaves with him
5		– one of Delaney's articles – here about coyotes
6	Kyra Delaney Neighbours	– Kyra supports idea of walling in Arroyo Blanco – Delaney is insecure about the topic, – seeing a Mexican in his street he becomes aggressive
7	Cándido América	– Cándido has been mugged, all their money is gone – they must eat food from a garbage bin
8	Delaney Kyra Cándido América	– Delaney has not fought the wall – he and Kyra go shopping for Thanksgiving – Cándido gets a free turkey at the supermarket, he hopes to liven up América now. When trying to cook it he sets the canyon on fire.

Part Three

1	Delaney Kyra	– Delaney, Kyra and her mother attend D. Flood's Thanksgiving party – party is disturbed by sirens of firefighters
2	Cándido Kyra	– Cándido and América barely escape the fire, unfortunately she feels the baby coming, Cándido looks for shelter and finds the maintenance shed of Arroyo Blanco
3	Delaney Kyra Neighbours	– Arroyo Blanco must be evacuated, when the crowd sees two Mexicans climbing up the canyon they turn into a mob. They can return home, Kyra's mother has been tricked by D. Flood.
4	América Cándido	– América gives birth to a daughter, Cándido builds a kind of hut for shelter, he cooks the Mossbachers' cat in a stew
5	Delaney Kyra	– the Da Ros place is a victim of the flames – there is Spanish graffiti on Arroyo Blanco's wall
6	Cándido América	– they have lost all their money in the fire, their daughter is blind, a heavy rain sets in, Cándido is recognized and attacked by Delaney.
7	Delaney Cándido	– Delaney's car is hit by a truck because he parked it wrongly – he follows Cándido on his own and wants to punish him
8	Delaney Cándido América	– Delaney finds Cándido and América in their hut and threatens them with his gun when a monstrous mudslide washes them all away, the daughter is killed, but Cándido saves Delaney from drowning

The Author

Tom Coraghessan Boyle was born in Peekskill (1948), a town in New York state located on the Hudson River. Boyle grew up in a working-class, Catholic family. Both his parents were alcoholics. His grandparents emigrated from Ireland and his father grew up in an orphanage. Although Boyle claims that he did not read fiction until he was eighteen, he recalls being intrigued by the newspaper stories his mother read to him. A self-proclaimed hellion who cut classes and abused drugs throughout his youth, he was much influenced by the hippie-ideals of the 1960s. After school he enrolled at the State University of New York at Potsdam intending to major in music, but "didn't have the discipline to do the practicing". He began writing as a junior at Potsdam, when he enrolled in a creative writing course. From 1964 to 1968, he was a student at Potsdam, where he majored in history and took a bevy of courses in English. While he was an undergraduate at Potsdam, Boyle took a number of history courses from Dr. Vincent J. Knapp. Following his graduation from college, Boyle taught high school English in Peekskill to avoid serving in Vietnam. During this interval he published his first short story, *"The OF & Hepatitis RR or Bust"* in *The North American Review*, and this piece won him admission to the University of Iowa Writers' Workshop. Once enrolled in the Workshop, Boyle became eligible to take classes in the English department and began work on a Ph.D. in literature. "The minute I got there," he once wrote, "I grew up. Instead of cutting classes, I sat in the front row and took notes." Although his declared speciality was the Victorian period, Boyle received his doctorate in 1977 for a collection of short fiction published two years later as *"Descent of Man, and Other Stories"*. Prior to 1988, he was relatively unknown. This was true even though he had published two books of short stories that were well received, and two novels, including a notable novel in 1982 titled *"Water Music"*. Boyle has explained that this novel "comes out of having done a Ph.D. in nineteenth-century British literature," citing the essays of John Ruskin and the novels of Charles Dickens as particular influences. His break-through came in 1988, when his third novel *"World's End"* won the PEN-Faulkner award as the best novel published that year in the United States. That novel was set in New York state. In terms of both critical and popular reception, it represented a watershed for Boyle. Recounting the tangled histories of three families living in the Hudson River valley, the narrative alternates between scenes featuring the seventeenth-century members of these clans and depictions of their descendants in the 1960s; the more recent passages also feature flashbacks to the 1920s and '30s. After receiving the prestigious award, his considerable literary talents were recognized throughout the country. And at that point, he truly became a cult writer, with a devoted group of readers. All of his books are in print, and 600,000 copies of his works are in book stores around the U.S. and internationally. Many of the motifs introduced in *"Descent of Man"* recur throughout his short fiction. One of these themes is his conviction that, beneath the technological innovations and ostensible sophistication of modern life, humans remain primitive beings who fall into one or two categories - predator or prey. Other themes in his short fiction include the tension between reason and instinct, the self-indulgent materialism that he considers endemic to consumer society and the jaded complacency that results, in his view, from media excesses. *"The Tortilla Curtain"* was published in 1995. Boyle currently teaches English and creative writing at the University of Southern California, Los Angeles. He lives with his family near Santa Barbara.

Vorüberlegungen zum Einsatz des Romans im Unterricht

Boyles Roman, erschienen 1995, eignet sich hervorragend als Schullektüre, da er sprachlich von Oberstufenkursen der 12. und 13. Jahrgangsstufe gut bewältigt werden kann. Der kontrastierende Aufbau des Romans, der die Problematik der illegalen Einwanderung von Mexikanern in die USA aus Sicht eines mexikanischen Paares, das unter menschenunwürdigen Bedingungen in einem Canyon haust, und aus Sicht eines weißen mittelständischen Paares beleuchtet, motiviert ständig zum Weiterlesen.

Die Thematik des Romans lässt sich vielfältig in das Oberstufencurriculum einbinden, z. B. im Rahmen einer Themenreihe zu *The American Dream, Minorities, Immigration and Multiculturalism, Politics* und *Bilingualism.* So könnte sich die Besprechung des Romans an eine Unterrichtsreihe *Hispanics in the USA* anschließen, die man mit dem Themenschwerpunkt *Bilingual or English-only Education* behandeln kann.

Der Roman hat einen Umfang von ca. 300 Seiten, daher kann kaum erwartet werden, dass alle Schülerinnen und Schüler ihn vor der Besprechung ganz lesen. Da er in drei Teile geteilt ist, sollte man den Schülerinnen und Schülern jeweils ca. 2-3 Wochen Lesezeit pro Teil einräumen, wobei die Interpretation des gesamten Werkes nach 2 Wochen Vorlaufzeit nicht mehr als 8 Schulwochen einnehmen sollte. Darüber hinaus werden wiederholende Leseaufträge für einzelne Kapitel gegeben, wenn diese detailliert besprochen werden sollen.

Zu diesem Roman gibt es bisher keine Unterrichtsmodelle, jedoch wurde er von Prof. Dr. Peter Freese (Universität Paderborn) in einer Lehrerfortbildung in Speyer im April 1999 vorgestellt und eingehend besprochen. Dabei stellte sich heraus, dass bereits mehrere Kolleginnen und Kollegen ihn mit Erfolg in ihren Oberstufenkursen gelesen hatten. Von Herrn Prof. Freese ist ein Aufsatz (T. Coraghessan Boyle's *The Torilla Curtain*: A Case Study in the Genesis of Xenophobia, in: *English Literatures in International Context*s, ed. by Heinz Antor/Klaus Stiersdorfer, Heidelberg: Carl Winter, 2000) veröffentlicht worden. T. C. Boyle ist zwar ein Bestsellerautor, wird jedoch von der „seriösen" Kritik größtenteils übergangen.

Es sind verschiedene Ausgaben des Romans auf dem Markt, die jedoch dieselbe Seitenzählung haben, sodass die Angaben des Unterrichtsmodells in jedem Fall übernommen werden können. Am preisgünstigsten sind die Taschenbuchausgaben, z.B. Bloomsbury, 1995 oder Penguin, 1996. Außerdem gibt es ein Audiobook: T. C. Boyle, The Tortilla Curtain. Read by the author. Audio Renaissance Tapes, 1995. Auf Deutsch ist das Buch unter dem Titel *América* erschienen (übersetzt von Werner Richter).

Klausuren

Im Folgenden werden zwei Klausurvorschläge zum Roman *The Tortilla Curtain* vorgestellt. Während die erste Klausur auf einer Textstelle im Roman basiert, besteht die zweite Klausur aus einem romantextunabhängigen nicht-fiktionalen Text, der sich um das Themengebiet *immigration* bewegt.
Die **Klausur 1** kann im Laufe der Lektüre des Romans gestellt werden, allerdings erst, nachdem die ersten beiden Teile des Romans vollständig und die Kapitel III.1 oder III.2 gelesen wurden. Ebenso sollten die ersten beiden Teile im Unterricht weitgehend bearbeitet worden sein. Es empfiehlt sich, den Schülerinnen und Schülern eine Kopie der Textstelle zur Verfügung zu stellen, wobei sie gleichzeitig mit ihrer Lektüre arbeiten können. Die Kopie dient der Möglichkeit, Passagen großzügig zu unterstreichen bzw. herauszuheben. Die Lektüre ist vor allem für *assignment 3* eine wichtige Grundlage. Die Klausur ist wahrscheinlich eher für einen Grundkurs geeignet. Wenn allerdings *assignment 5* durch eine kritische Stellungnahme zur Kritik *Snobs and Wetbacks* (siehe *Component 4*) ersetzt wird, kann sie auch als Klausur für einen Leistungskurs vorgesehen werden.
Es empfiehlt sich, dass **Klausur 2**, im Gegensatz zu Klausur 1, erst nach der vollständigen Lektüre des Romans gestellt wird. Obwohl der zugrunde liegende Text vom Romantext unabhängig ist, bezieht er sich dennoch auf viele Aspekte des Themas der illegalen Immigration. Die Ergebnisse der Besprechung des Romans sind von Bedeutung, weil die Schüler in der Klausur aufgefordert werden, den Themenkomplex aus eigener Sicht zu beleuchten bzw. eigenes Wissen einzubringen. Es ist jedoch nicht notwendig, dass die Schüler ihre Lektüre zur Verfügung haben. Diese Klausur ist für einen Grundkurs gut geeignet. Je nach Könnensstand und Alter der Lerngruppe kann der Aufgabenapparat selbstverständlich gekürzt werden.

Notizen:

Text: Excerpt from *The Tortilla Curtain* by T. C. Boyle (p. 286, l. 12 to p. 290, l. 2)

Assignments

1. In the first chapter of the book Delaney is introduced as a liberal humanist. In this excerpt he behaves completely differently. Find passages in which his racist behaviour becomes obvious. Give reasons for this change.

2. The crowd which has gathered at the top of Topanga Canyon consists of affluent civilized Anglo-American people. Identify the factors that turn them into an uninhibited mob when they face the two Mexicans.

3. José Navidad is one of the two Mexicans walking up the road. Explain his behaviour towards the Anglo-Americans in this excerpt. To what extent is he different from Cándido and América, the other two Mexicans that play an important role in the book? Comment on these differences using the whole novel as a basis.

4. Identify some stylistic devices Boyle uses to express Delaney's and the crowd's anger and hatred when confronting the two Mexicans.

5. Imagine you are the Hispanic cop who arrested the two Mexicans. The following day you meet a friend to whom you describe the entire incident with the two Mexicans and the Anglo-American crowd.

Erwartungshorizont zu Klausur 1

zu 1: Delaney is full of hatred when he sees the two Latinos. He tells the police a lie by claiming that he saw José in the canyon where the fire started. When the Mexican spits at him, Delaney attacks him without any restraint. He does not convey any sense of remorse or guilt. Several reasons for this change can be mentioned: an accumulation of unfortunate events related to Mexicans such as Delaney's car hitting Cándido / the theft of his car / Kyra's fear of encountering the Latinos at the Da Ros place and the argument about the wall between Delaney and Kyra / Delaney's consumption of alcohol / the Arroyo Blanco inhabitants turning into a mob under the influence of alcohol and rage / the raging fire / the deep-rooted fear of losing their possessions.

zu 2: They turn into an uninhibited mob for several reasons: people are under the influence of alcohol / deep-rooted fear of the raging fire / extreme anxiety about their belongings and houses / their subliminal prejudices against Latinos have always been there and are fully released now / they obviously have a psychological need to find a scapegoat, and the two Mexicans suitably meet this need.

zu 3: José shows a behaviour full of spite and contempt for Anglos. When encountering the crowd he does not display any haste or agitation, but coolness and impassiveness. He wants to show them that he is not interested in their concerns. When he feels Delaney's hateful look resting on him, he is not submissive or intimidated, on the contrary, he becomes offensive and spits at him. His hate results in the threatening phrase "I kill you, motherfucker!" (p. 289, l. 16f.)
América and Cándido are extremely submissive towards all Anglo-Americans and do not revolt against their predicament. They are nourished by their dream of a better life (apartment, garden, TV, etc) which makes them bear even the most terrible circumstances. They take any kind of work for little money: América cleaning the buddhas with a toxic detergent / Cándido is pushed away like a dog in the parking lot of the supermarket without showing any resistance (p. 105) / América lets her employer grab at her without complaining (p. 97). In contrast to them José displays constant aggressiveness and suspicion. His underprivileged situation has fed his hate towards all Anglos. He acts violently when he is refused at the labour exchange (p. 82) / when encountering Delaney in the canyon (p. 117) and Kyra on the Da Ros property (p. 164f.) he puts on an indifferent and even mocking manner imposing some kind of menace / he is not even loyal to his own countrymen, interfering with América and finally raping her (p. 82f. / p. 141f.)

zu 4: **Climactic structure**
"This was the jerk with the "flies", the wiseass, the camper." (p. 286, l. 19f.)
"The son of a bitch. The jerk, The arsonist." (p. 288, l. 25)
"..., but this time Delaney didn't flinch, didn't feel guilt or pity or even the slightest tug of common humanity." (p. 289, l. 6f.)
"..., fists clenched, ready to go anywhere, do anything, seething with it, spoiling for it, a mob." (p. 289, l. 31f.)

Metaphor
"... his voice a magnificent trumpeting instrument". (p. 287, l. 33)
"... a cacophony of threats and name-calling." (p. 289, l. 20 f.)

Simile
"The smoke lay on the air like poison, like doom." (p. 289, l. 29)

zu 5: The pupils should try to identify with the Hispanic cop in an authentic manner. They should therefore comment on his feelings about having to arrest two Hispanics and about the reaction of the angry mob. They should also present a plausible and convincing point of view of his role as a Hispanic cop in a police force having to defend white Anglos' rights and pursue illegal Mexican immigrants. This might create an inner conflict in him.

Notizen:

California turns against its force of Latin labourers

Report by Phil Reeves in Los Angeles

The scene is the same every morning. As the sun rises over the mountains of southern California, scores of bedraggled-looking Latino men gather on street corners in the suburbs of Los Angeles, and watch the rest of America drive to work. They are standing there, smoking cigarettes and chatting softly among themselves, in the hope that they will be recruited as temporary manual labourers.

Every so often, a smart-looking Jeep or a Ford Bronco pulls up and one of the waiting crowd is spirited off for a day clearing a garden in Los Angeles, shifting lumber in Ventura, or pruning bushes on a golf course in Palm Springs. After a few hours, the rest wander home, only to return the following day in the hope that they will be chosen.

Many of the men – Mexicans, Salvadoreans, Guatemalans and others – are members of California's 2.1 million population of illegal immigrants, most of whom have slipped across California's southern border with Mexico in search of dollars to send home. For years they have been tolerated by the resident population, although never much liked. Now the mood has changed; they have become the target of one of the toughest recent measures against illegal immigration drafted in an American state, laws that some predict will set a pattern nation-wide.

On 8 November, Californians will decide by public ballot whether to strip illegal immigrants of their rights to non-emergency health care, welfare services, and education for their children.

The measure would compel state officials, including teachers and health workers, to "snitch" on anyone they suspected of being in the US illegally. If a Mexican child appears to have undocumented parents, his teachers would be obliged by law to pick up the telephone to the US Immigration and Naturalisation Service. "It is the police state mentality," Al Lundeen, one of the principal opponents, said.

Despite such draconian terms, the proposal – known as Proposition 187 – has won considerable support in California, even among elements of the Latino population. In the past few years the Golden State, once seen as the engine that drove the vast US economy, has seen the worst slump since the Great Depression. Not least because of deep post-Cold War cuts in the defence and aerospace industry. As jobs have become increasingly scarce, an anti-immigrant mood has uncoiled ...

The proponents of the measure – which they call the Save Our State initiative – argue it will make life so uncomfortable for illegal immigrants that they will eventually return home, reliev-

bedraggled untidy, dirty

to predict to foresee

ballot a secret vote

Proposition *„Vorlage für einen Volksentscheid"*

the Golden State = California

slump time when there is a lot of unemployment and poverty in a country

ing an annual burden of around $3bn on Californian taxpayers; who have grown tired of paying for their schooling, their health care, and their crimes (there are some 16,000 illegal immigrants in California's prisons).
However, the figures are much disputed ... Nor is it clear whether the proposal, if passed, would be legal. A decision by the US Supreme Court in 1982 outlawed denying a public school education to any American child, whether he be in the country legally or not.
In reality, the issue has more to do with politics than with economics. The prevailing hostility towards illegal immigrants has been seized upon and stoked up by the state's politicians, who have made it a central theme in the forthcoming mid-term elections. [...]

to outlaw to make illegal

Assignments

1. Describe the situation illegal immigrants in California are confronted with.

2. Why has Proposition 187 "won considerable support in California" (l. 34)?

3. Characterize the text type the author employs to oppose Proposition 187.

4. Give a personal evaluation of Proposition 187 taking the political situation in the USA into account.

Erwartungshorizont zu Klausur 2

zu 1: In the past illegal Hispanic immigrants could find temporary jobs and were tolerated by the resident Californians. Now, however, they see themselves confronted with an impending proposition which would deprive them of certain rights (health care, welfare services, education for their children). These measures would make life almost impossible for the illegal immigrants in California (and eventually make them leave the country).

zu 2: The author mentions economic and political reasons. California is going through "the worst slump since the great Depression" (l. 37 f.) and the illegal immigrants are held responsible for the high rate of unemployment. The Californians are no longer willing to pay for the immigrants' health care, education and crimes. Politicians have made the problem a central theme in the forthcoming elections.

zu 3: This argumentative text reports on an impending proposition which is being discussed very controversially. The author is clearly against this proposal and tries to convince the reader of his opinion by first giving more information on illegal immigrants. (He describes their marginal position in American society which becomes obvious when they offer themselves for jobs, and lets the reader know where they come from and why they left their home countries.) Then he points out that Proposition 187 would deprive them of their rights. He adds arguments of the supporters of Proposition 187, but also gives counter-arguments. At the end the author mentions two important arguments against the proposition: it is not clear that the passing of this proposition would be legal and the fact that politicians have made this problem a central theme in the forthcoming elections.

zu 4: Since the assignment requires a personal comment, the evaluation can be positive or negative. Arguments in favour: high rate of unemployment, high number of illegal immigrants and their expensive crimes. Arguments against: plight of the immigrants, their exploitation, history of America as a nation of immigrants.

Notizen:

Konzeption des Unterrichtsmodells

Der Roman *The Tortilla Curtain* wird sicherlich seinen Platz im Oberstufenunterricht deutscher Schulen finden. Boyle zwingt die Leserschaft, sich mit dem Problem illegaler Einwanderung und Minderheiten auseinander zu setzen, ohne einseitig auf Mitleid für die *minorities* abzuzielen. Durch Delaneys schwankende Haltung ist man aufgefordert, darüber nachzudenken, wie man selbst an seiner Stelle reagieren würde. Diese Auseinandersetzung führt zu Überlegungen, wie in Deutschland mit Minderheiten umgegangen wird, und somit ist der Bezug zu den Lebensumständen der Schülerinnen und Schüler gegeben.

Das vorliegende Unterrichtsmodell will die verschiedenen Aspekte der illegalen Einwanderung aus den im Roman vorgestellten Perspektiven vertiefen. Es bietet sowohl textanalytische Interpretationen als auch kreative und handlungsorientierte Aufgaben.

Die Dreiteilung des Romans legt es nahe, den Schülerinnen und Schülern nicht alle 350 Seiten auf einmal als Leseaufgabe zu stellen, sondern die Lesearbeit in drei Teile aufzuteilen. Die Unglücksfälle, die die Protagonisten heimsuchen, werden von Kapitel zu Kapitel verheerender, Delaneys Haltung wird immer radikaler, Cándido und América werden immer verzweifelter.

Der Schwerpunkt der Interpretation liegt auf der Betrachtung von Delaneys Entwicklung und der Frage, wie jemand, der sich selbst als Liberaler bezeichnet, innerhalb weniger Monate zum Reaktionär wird. Daneben wird untersucht, wie die Verzweiflung und der Glaube an den *American Dream* Cándido und América dazu treiben, unter menschenunwürdigen Verhältnissen monatelang unter freiem Himmel zu kampieren.

Die *Components* folgen dem Verlauf des Romans und sollten daher nicht in ihrer Reihenfolge umgestellt werden. Innerhalb der *Components* werden unterschiedliche Schwerpunkte gesetzt, Aufgabenstellungen und Arbeitsformen variieren. Wortfeldarbeit, stilistische Analyse und Interpretation von Statistiken werden ebenso berücksichtigt wie kreative Aufgaben.

Zu den angesprochenen Problemstellungen werden Arbeitsblätter und Tafelbilder bereitgestellt, sodass das Modell direkt in den Unterricht einbezogen werden kann. Je nach Bedarf können einzelne Punkte ausgelassen, erweitert oder in Klausuren verwendet werden. Die Bearbeitung eines *Components* erfordert mehrere Unterrichtsstunden, Piktogramme am Rand erleichtern eine schnelle Orientierung über Leitfragen, Sozial- und Arbeitsformen sowie kreative Ansätze. Aufgaben, die sich zur häuslichen Bearbeitung anbieten, sind besonders gekennzeichnet.

Man kann als begleitende Aufgabe einzelne Schülerinnen und Schüler auffordern, pro Kapitel eine kurze Zusammenfassung zu schreiben, die dann in der Klasse zur Orientierung aller in der richtigen Reihenfolge an der Wand aufgehängt werden. Außerdem bietet es sich an, jeweils einer Schülerin / einem Schüler die Aufgabe zu stellen, 10–15 wichtige Vokabeln aus je einem Kapitel herauszusuchen, die dann als Lernvokabular oder als Hilfen dem gesamten Kurs zur Verfügung gestellt werden können.

Die **Einstiegsseite** des Unterrichtsmodells sollte auf Folie kopiert werden und dient dazu, einen motivierenden Einstieg in den Roman zu bieten. Dies sollte auch erfolgen, wenn die Thematik bereits über Sachtexte dem Kurs vorgestellt wurde.

In **Component 1**, bezogen auf *Part One* werden die Protagonisten mit ihren unterschiedlichen Lebensumständen und Einstellungen vorgestellt. Der Schwerpunkt liegt dabei auf Delaneys Grundhaltung gegenüber der der anderen Weißen in seinem Lebensumfeld. An Aufgabenschwerpunkten finden sich Wortfeldarbeit *migration, point of view* und Interpretation von Statistiken. *Point of view* ist in diesem Zusammenhang ein interessanter Aspekt, da er in *The Tortilla Curtain* ständig wechselt. Hier wird untersucht, inwiefern die Erzählperspektive den Leser beeinflusst.

Component 2, ebenfalls bezogen auf *Part One*, untersucht schwerpunktmäßig die Symbole, die T. C. Boyle in seinem Roman benutzt. Dabei sollen die Schülerinnen und Schüler dafür sensibilisiert werden, dass hinter der offenkundigen Handlung oftmals eine versteckte Ebene liegt.

In **Component 3**, bezogen auf *Part Two*, liegt ein Schwerpunkt auf der Stilanalyse von Textausschnitten. Die Berührungspunkte zwischen Weißen und Mexikanern werden genauer untersucht. Die Interpretation der Symbole, die in *Component 2* vorgestellt wurden, wird wieder aufgenommen.

Component 4, bezogen auf *Part One, Two and Three*, untersucht Delaneys Entwicklung zum Radikalen im Verlauf des gesamten Romans, der eine Waffe in die Hand nimmt, um die Illegalen zu vertreiben. Die Symbole der beiden ersten Teile werden weiterverfolgt.

Am Ende des Unterrichtsmodells befindet sich ein **Glossar**, das häufig auftretende spanische Ausdrücke enthält. Auf Zusatztexte wurde innerhalb der *Components* verzichtet, da es zu dem Thema *Hispanics/Minorities* von verschiedenen Verlagen Themenhefte gibt und der Roman mit einem Umfang von 350 Seiten ausreichend Lesestoff bietet. Neben amerikanischen Tageszeitungen und Wochenmagazinen bietet auch das Internet eine Menge von aktuellen Informationen. Eine **Zusammenstellung von Textquellen und Webseitenadressen** findet sich im Anhang, die eine Vielfalt von Möglichkeiten der Einbettung des Romans in den Themenkomplex bietet.

Component 1: When Worlds Clash

1.1 First encounter and clashes between the two worlds

Der erste *Component* beschäftigt sich mit der Erarbeitung des ersten Teils des Romans. Dabei werden zwei Hauptaspekte beleuchtet, zum einen die Erstbegegnung der beiden Welten mit der sich dabei ergebenden Problematik der illegalen Einwanderung in die USA und zum anderen die unterschiedlichen Sichtweisen und Haltungen einiger zentraler Figuren zur Einwanderung im Allgemeinen.
Voraussetzung für die erste Stunde ist, dass *Part I* des Buches ganz gelesen wurde, die Kapitel I.1, I.3, I.6 und I.7 intensiv, die anderen extensiv.
Für den Einstieg werden zwei unterschiedliche Verfahren vorgeschlagen. Erstens kann man mit den Schülerinnen und Schülern ein Wortfeld zum Thema *migration* erarbeiten, das einige der Bereiche mit den dazugehörigen Wendungen und Wörtern enthält, die in der vorhergegangenen Unterrichtsreihe schon erarbeitet worden sind. Dieses Wortfeld kann auf verschiedene Arten entwickelt werden, entweder als *mind map* an der Tafel oder auf Folie, in Gruppen- oder Partnerarbeit. Eine weitere Variante besteht darin, dass man das Wortfeld in Form einer Wandzeitung entwickelt, die im Verlaufe der Unterrichtsreihe weiter mit Inhalten gefüllt werden kann, abhängig davon, ob entsprechendes Vokabular in einem Kapitel vorkommt oder nicht.
Selbstverständlich ist das Erstellen einer *mind map* eine ganz offene Aufgabe, die stark von den Schülern gelenkt wird. Dennoch ergeben sich etliche Begriffe im Zusammenhang mit *migration* relativ logisch und zwingend. Deshalb sei die folgende Struktur einer *mind map* vorgegeben, welche die Schüler dann auf *Worksheet 1* mit geeigneten Begriffen füllen können. Vorschläge für Wörter und Wendungen zu den einzelnen Themenbereichen sind im Anschluss angegeben.

Develop a mind map woven around "migration".

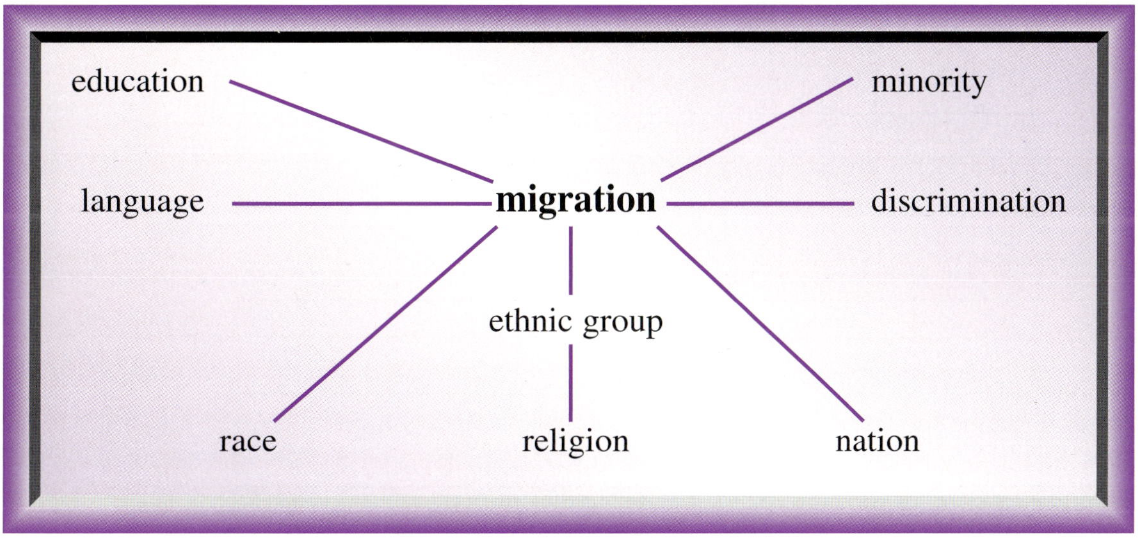

Word Field "Migration"

Develop a word field referring to "migration".

migration – ______________________________

____

education – ______________________________

____

language – ______________________________

____

minority – ______________________________

____

discrimination – ______________________________

____

ethnic group – ______________________________

____

race – ______________________________

____

religion – ______________________________

____

nation – ______________________________

____

Lösungsvorschlag zu Worksheet 1

migration
immigrant
immigration
to immigrate into
emigrant
emigration
to emigrate from
exile
immigration and language policies
a backlash against immigrants
person seeking asylum
applicant for asylum
to grant asylum
to be granted a work permit
influx of illegal immigrants
economic refugee
to absorb a new surge of immigrants
to naturalize
naturalization

minority
to outnumber sb
to be in the majority / minority
to integrate sb into society
to encourage / discourage
integration / segregation
to adapt to new surroundings
to adopt different customs
protection of minority rights

ethnic group
to exacerbate ethnic tensions
mixed marriages
ethnic, cultural diversity
melting pot
acculturation
Americanisation
assimilation, to assimilate
to cling to one's ethnicity

religion
Protestant, Catholic
Muslim, Jew
Mormon, Baptist
denomination
to practise a distinctive religion

education
to restrict bilingual education programs
to raise / to lower the educational level

language
official language
resentment toward non-English speakers
linguistic unit
primacy of English
to eliminate non-English voting ballots
to tighten language-proficiency standards
bilingualism
institutionalized language
survey of language attitudes
segregation
language assistance
loss of national unity

discrimination
to be / to feel inferior / superior to
to regard as second-class citizens
to live in ghettos
privileged / underprivileged
disadvantaged
bigotry
to be discriminated against
to fight for civil rights
to discourage prejudice
to be prejudiced against

race
Asian, white, black, negro
coloured people
racial issue
multiracial society
racism, racist, racial hatred
to carry out a racial policy
racial problems arise
race relations improve / deteriorate
race riots break out
to hold racist views
to persecute / persecution

nation
German, Irish, Chinese
to become integrated into national life

Zweitens könnte man die Schülerinnen und Schüler mit der am Anfang dieses Buches vorgestellten Collage mit Szenen und Bildern aus dem Süden Kaliforniens als Folie konfrontieren und sie dazu spontan Stellung nehmen lassen. Die Collage bietet sich auch als stummer Impuls an.

Look at this picture. What is shown here? Comment on the function of the fence. What does the pictograph of the three people (man, woman and child) express?

Bei der Besprechung der Collage werden von den Schülern und Schülerinnen sicherlich Kenntnisse und Ergebnisse aus der vorhergegangenen Unterrichtsreihe eingebracht, z.B. Wissen über die hispanische Immigration in die USA sowie über die aktuelle themenbezogene politische Diskussion und über die spezifische geographische Situation in dem betreffenden Landstrich.
Im Anschluss an die Besprechung der Collage kann mit der Lerngruppe gemeinsam der Inhalt des ersten Kapitels von *Part I* zusammengefasst werden, was mündlich ohne unterstützenden Tafelanschrieb geschehen kann.
Daraufhin wird die Aufmerksamkeit der Schüler auf die Figur des Delaney gelenkt. Man kann mit folgender Fragestellung fortfahren:

What information does the reader get about Delaney? (Chapter I.1)

- D. is a man who lives in California close to the Mexican border with his wife and son (p. 3 / p. 14f.)
- takes bottles to the recycler's (p. 3) and is outraged at the trash produced in the countryside

⇒ environmentally friendly

- when he hits the Mexican he comes into conflict with his liberal humanist attitude (p. 10f.)
- first he offers to take the Mexican to a doctor, then he only gives him some money (p. 8f.)
- D. does not report the accident to the police
- D. lies to the car dealer (p. 13)
- D. is surprised to see Mexicans working at the recycler's (p. 11f.)

Als Hausaufgabe zur nächsten Stunde sollen die Schülerinnen und Schüler die Informationen zur Person des Delaney in einem geschlossenen Text formulieren und eine summary von Kapitel 6 erstellen.

Write a short text about Delaney using all the information we have collected in class.

Nachdem die Hausaufgabe kurz vorgetragen wurde, wird der Text von Seite 7, Zeile 3 bis Seite 9, Zeile 13 von einem Schüler oder einer Schülerin vorgelesen. Die Diskussion wird wieder auf die Figur des Delaney gelenkt, der am Anfang des Buches als *liberal humanist* bezeichnet wird. Nun wird Delaney's Verhalten nach dem Unfall herausgearbeitet. Beide Aspekte können unter der folgenden Fragestellung im Unterrichtsgespräch behandelt werden.

Explain the discrepancy between Delaney's ideals and his behaviour after the accident. (Chapter 1)

Die Ergebnisse lassen sich kurz an der Tafel festhalten:

Discrepancy between Delaney's ideals and his behaviour after the accident

- liberal-humanist ideals (p. 3)
- feelings of pity for the desperate situation of the Mexican (p. 9)
- environmentally-friendly person

versus

- D. does not call an ambulance, but gives money to the Mexican (p. 9)
- feeling of outrage against the Hispanics polluting the environment
- lies to the car dealer about the cause of the accident

Das Unterrichtsgespräch wendet sich José Navidad zu. Da die Hausaufgabe darin bestand, den Inhalt des Kapitels 6 zusammenzufassen, können nun ausgehend von diesem Kapitel charakteristische Merkmale von José herausgearbeitet werden. Folgende Fragestellung kann sich ergeben:

José Navidad is another central character among the Mexicans. What are his characteristic features? (Chapter I.6)

Die Bearbeitung dieser Aufgabe kann in arbeitsteiliger Gruppenarbeit erfolgen. Die eine Gruppe legt das Augenmerk auf *outward appearance*, die andere auf *behaviour*. Die Ergebnisse lassen sich folgendermaßen an der Tafel festhalten:

Characteristic features of José Navidad

a) outward appearance
- hard unblinking eyes (p. 81); jabbing out at the world like two weapons (p. 81)
- dentures; something rotting inside of him (p. 82)
- baseball cap turned backwards (p. 88)

⇒ filthy and shabby impression

b) behaviour
- acts violently when refused at the labour exchange; no patience (p. 82)
- approaches América in an aggressive and intrusive manner (p. 82f.)
- shows curiosity towards Cándido and questions him (p. 89)
- embodies a menace to Cándido (p. 90)

⇒ displays aggressiveness and suspicion

Nachdem José Navidad näher beleuchtet wurde, bietet es sich an, die beiden zentralen mexikanischen Figuren, Cándido und América, in den Blickpunkt zu rücken. Auf der Grundlage der Kapitel 1 und 6 kann erst einmal allgemein herausgearbeitet werden, dass die Persönlichkeiten von América und Cándido auf der einen und José auf der anderen Seite recht konträr sind. Ebenso differieren ihre Haltungen zu den spezifischen Lebensbedingungen und Herausforderungen nach der Flucht in die USA gewaltig. Da die Hausaufgabe darin bestand, Kapitel 6 zusammenzufassen, bietet es sich an, zunächst die Person der América unter folgender Aufgabenstellung zu beleuchten:

Work out the attitudes of Cándido, América and José towards the living and working conditions in the US and the American people they encounter. (Chapter I.1; Chapter I.6)

Es ergibt sich etwa folgender Tafelanschrieb:

Attitudes towards life in the USA and the Americans

América

- takes any kind of work for little money (p. 84)
- works extremely hard to make a good impression (in contrast to the American woman) (p. 93f.)
- lets her employer grab at her without complaining (p. 97)
- stealing is something immoral to her which she only does in an extreme emergency (p. 60)

Die beiden anderen Figuren können in der folgenden Stunde unter diesem Aspekt beleuchtet werden. Diese Aufgabenstellung kann auch als Hausaufgabe gegeben werden. Falls ausreichend Zeit vorhanden ist, kann man die Betrachtung der beiden anderen Figuren noch in diese Stunde mit hineinnehmen. Es bietet sich an, als Hausaufgabe eine *creative writing*-Aufgabe zu stellen, bei der die Schülerinnen und Schüler gehalten sind, sich näher mit der Person der América auseinander zu setzen, indem sie versuchen, sich in sie hineinzuversetzen. Man könnte sich folgende Fragestellung vorstellen:

Put yourself in América's position and describe in an interior monologue how you reacted to Cándido's accident and the experiences and feelings you had when you found your first job. (Chapter I.1; Chapter I.6)

Bei der Bearbeitung dieser Aufgabe kommt es darauf an, dass die Schüler die Fakten korrekt wiedergeben und die Gefühle und Stimmungen der Person der América authentisch beschreiben.

In der folgenden Stunde werden die beiden anderen mexikanischen Figuren hinsichtlich ihrer Haltung zu den Lebensumständen und Herausforderungen ihrer neuen Umgebung behandelt.

What are Cándido's and José's attitudes towards life in the US and the Americans? (Chapter I.1; Chapter I.6)

Es kann sich folgender Tafelanschrieb ergeben:

Attitude towards their new lives

Cándido
- takes any kind of work for little money
- is prepared to work hard to make a good impression (p. 80)
- never complains or shouts at Americans (p. 7f., 92)
- never tries to take advantage of a situation (p. 7f.)

⇒ both Cándido and América are willing to bear any hardship and suffering in order to stay in the US

José
- defiant attitude towards the headman (p. 82)
- is not willing to wait patiently for his turn (p. 82)
- the submissive position he had to take towards whites has made him evil (p. 81)
- talks to Cándido in an intrusive and menacing manner (p. 88f.)
- baseball cap turned backwards indicates an obstinate attitude towards the poor circumstances he lives in

⇒ openly shows his loathing of his poor circumstances

Im Anschluss an die Betrachtung der drei Mexikaner kann eine kurze Einführung bzw. Wiederholung des Komplexes *point of view* erfolgen. Zuerst werden die verschiedenen Varianten von *point of view* vorgestellt, daraufhin das erste Kapitel auf den hier vorliegenden *point of view* untersucht. Das folgende *Worksheet* fasst kurz die Informationen zum Thema zusammen.

Notizen:

Point of View

Whenever an author tells a story there must be a story teller. The story teller is not identical with the author; rather the author chooses a narrator who can tell the story from different angles, i.e. points of view. In the following the three most essential points of view are explained:

I. First-person narrator (limited)

The first-person narrator is a character inside the story. He/she can only inform about what he/she knows, feels, thinks and experiences. The narrator can be either a main character or a minor character. Because of the narrator's direct reporting of anything that happens the reader feels as close to the protagonist as the narrator does. It is easy for the reader to identify with the narrator.

II. Third-person narrator (selective-omniscient author)

The third-person author presents things as they are seen through the eyes of one or several characters in the story. He chooses to describe the thoughts and emotions of only one or several characters. The reader does not feel as close to the protagonists because the narrator tells the story in the third-person. He can only identify with those acting persons to whose consciousness the perspective is limited.

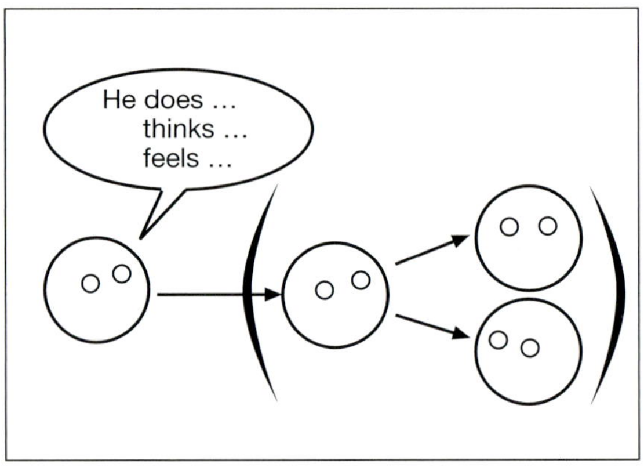

III. Third-person narrator (omniscient author)

An omniscient narrator can move freely in time and space. He can shift from character to character, reporting what he chooses of their speech, actions, thoughts, feelings and emotions. He may give comments or decide to show the action without judgement. This perspective enables the narrator to know everything and to enter the minds of all the characters. The reader can easily identify with the acting persons. But he does not feel spoken to as for instance when a first-person narrator tells a story.

Grafik: Víctor Prischtt

Nach der gemeinsamen Erarbeitung von *Worksheet 2* bieten sich folgende Aufgabenstellungen als Hausaufgabe an.

1. Analyse the narrator's point of view in Chapter I.1.
2. Tell the story in Chapter I.1 from Cándido's point of view.

Es wird etwa folgendes Ergebnis erwartet:

1. The narrator tells his story through Delaney's eyes. The reader learns everything about Delaney's feelings and emotions, but sees only what Delaney observes about other people. So there is a third-person selective-omniscient author. As the reader you can easily identify with Delaney since his feelings and emotions after the accident are conveyed to you very clearly.

Bei der zweiten Aufgabe kommt es darauf an, dass alle Tatsachen korrekt angesprochen werden und Cándidos eigenes Erleben möglichst authentisch wiedergegeben wird. Eine mögliche Lösung wäre die folgende Schülerarbeit aus einem 12. Jahrgang:

2. I had a really nasty experience. Maybe you think I'm insane, but I don't mind, I need to tell you, really, ... About a month ago I went to the labour exchange, but as usual there was no work for me, you know what I'm talking about. Then I went over to the supermarket to get some nachos and something to drink. I spent my last bucks on these.
   After that, carrying the shopping bag, I made my way back to the camp in the canyon. When I crossed the street and was trying to reach the other side one of those gringo cars faced me, a pile of chrome and metal.
   I couldn't even think of escaping that monstrous mass, then I found myself on the hood, and bounced right into the shrubs. That hit me hard, man! Gave me a beating I'll never forget! When I regained consciousness I stared right into the face of that gringo, you know, one of those pencil-pusher guys ...
   He was mumbling something like calling a doctor, but my body felt like I had been run over by a steamroller. There was pain in every limb of my body. How did that guy manage to ram into me!
   Right when I crossed the street that paranoid rushed round the corner, I mean, why didn't he see me? You usually see somebody crossing the street, unless you are blind but I think that guy wasn't blind because otherwise he wouldn't be allowed to drive. I bet he dreamed of his promotion or how he was going to wash and wax his car, those gringos always do! And when he was dreaming, he suddenly heard a loud noise, something like a muffled thump which was me, crushed onto the hood.
   The only thing they've got in mind is money, possession, influence, ... pinche pendejos! Do you know what he gave me as a compensation, you know that? He gave me 20 bucks for crippling me!
   I mean, what am I supposed to do now? América is pregnant and I need to recover. Does that guy really think that $ 20 are enough to pay for the destruction of the lives of three human beings? I'm so sorry for you gringos, I'd rather be a wreck than be as vile as you.

Um den zweiten Aspekt des ersten *Component* einzuleiten, die Haltung einiger zentraler Figuren zur Einwanderungsproblematik, bietet es sich an, zunächst eine Schülerin oder einen Schüler ein Kurzreferat zum Thema *Immigration into the US from the end of the 19th century until today* halten zu lassen. Als Grundlage für ein solches Referat eignet sich zum Beispiel ein Ausschnitt aus den Materialien vom Stark Verlag: Englisch – Unterrichtsmaterialien für Lehrkräfte Sekundarstufe II – Themenkreis „Landeskunde USA“ (Register M) *Immigration in America.*

Darüber hinaus befindet sich am Ende dieses Unterrichtsmodells ein Anhang mit Internet-Adressen zum Thema „Immigration in die USA“.
Nach dem Referat besteht noch die Möglichkeit, die am Ende dieses *Components* angegebenen Statistiken vom *U.S. Census Bureau* (*Worksheet 3* und *4*) zusammen mit den Schülern auszuwerten. Dabei werden die Fähigkeiten der Schüler, mit statistischem Material umzugehen und daraus Folgerungen abzuleiten, herausgefordert.

1.2 Conflicting points of view towards the immigration issue

Als Einstieg in den zweiten Teil des *Components* kann man von den Schülern den Abschnitt von S. 41, Z. 28 bis S. 45, Z. 31 vorlesen lassen. Dann wird die Diskussion auf die unterschiedlichen Haltungen zur Errichtung eines bewachten Eingangstors gelenkt, die von verschiedenen Bewohnern repräsentiert werden.

Discuss the attitudes of the residents to the building of a gate. (Chapter I.3)

Folgendes Tafelbild kann sich ergeben:

Illustration of the various opinions voiced during the meeting of the residents

a) Jim Shirley
   - houses broken into after a fixed pattern (p. 42f.)

   ⇒ emphasis on the security of the residents

b) athlete
   - prefers an open community with no fences, not only for privileged people (p. 43)

   ⇒ no elitist behaviour or discrimination of any group

c) Jack Cherrystone
   - basically wants to live humanist ideals but as the world is in such an immoral state he thinks it is naive to do so
   - therefore he favours the gate as something vital (p. 44)

   ⇒ disillusion about the outside world: secluded community important to live freely

d) Delaney
   - tries to voice his disapproval of the residents' tendency to feed coyotes and other wild animals (p. 44f.)

   ⇒ nature lover's point of view

Als Hausaufgabe zu dieser Stunde eignet sich z. B. die Bearbeitung der beiden folgenden *Worksheets.* Des Weiteren ist zu Kapitel 7 eine *summary* zu erstellen.

Worksheet 3

Immigration and economic development

Chart 1

Country of origin and year of entry into the U.S. of the foreign born, by Citizenship Status: March 1997 (Numbers in thousands)	Total Foreign-born		Naturalized Citizen		Not U.S. Citizen	
	Number	Percent	Number	Percent	Number	Percent
Country of Origin						
All countries	25,779	100.0	9,043	100.0	16.736	100.0
Mexico	7,017	27.2	1,044	11.5	5,973	35.7
Cuba	913	3.5	474	5.2	440	2.6
Dominican Republic	632	2.5	195	2.2	437	2.6
El Salvador	607	2.4	110	1.2	497	3.0
Great Britain	606	2.4	237	2.6	369	2.2
China and Hong Kong	1,107	4.3	536	5.9	570	3.4
India	748	2.9	263	2.9	485	2.9
Korea	591	2.3	220	2.4	372	2.2
Philippines	1,132	4.4	657	7.3	475	2.8
Vietnam	770	3.0	385	4.3	385	2.3
Elsewhere	11,655	45.2	4,921	54.4	6,734	40.2
Came to the United States						
All years of entry	25,779	100.0	9,043	100.0	16,736	100.0
Before 1970	4,749	18.4	3,523	39.0	1,226	7.3
1970 to 1979	4,935	19.1	2,580	28.5	2,356	14.1
1980 to 1989	8,555	33.2	2,414	26.7	6,141	36.7
Since 1990	7,539	29.2	526	5.8	7,013	41.9

Source: March 1997 Current Population Survey, U.S. Census Bureau

Chart 2

Economic development in Mexico 1930–1993

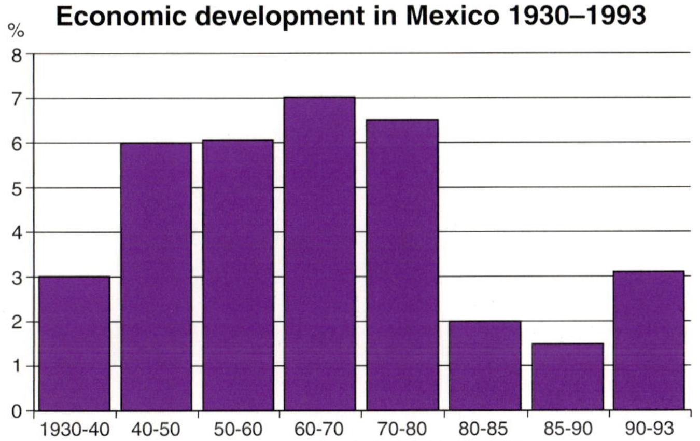

Source: Nohlen/Nuscheler 1992, 175 und Länderbericht Mexiko 1995

Chart 3

Demographic development in California and Mexico

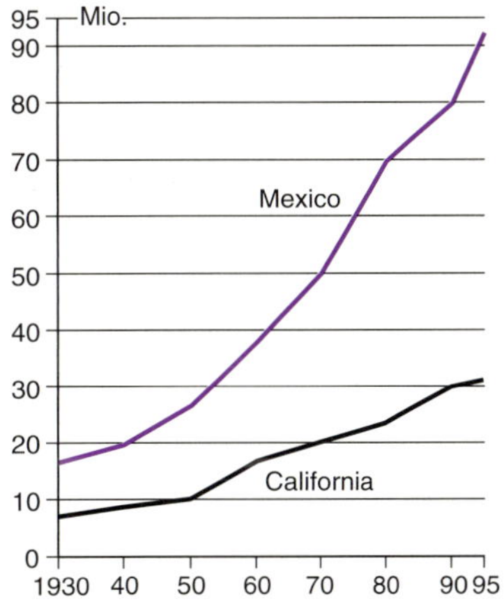

Source: Länderbericht USA 1994 und Mexiko 1995

1. Describe the development of immigration into and naturalization in the USA.
2. Try to find reasons for the rising numbers of Mexican immigrants taking into consideration the information given in charts 2 and 3.

Proportion of Hispanics

Chart 4

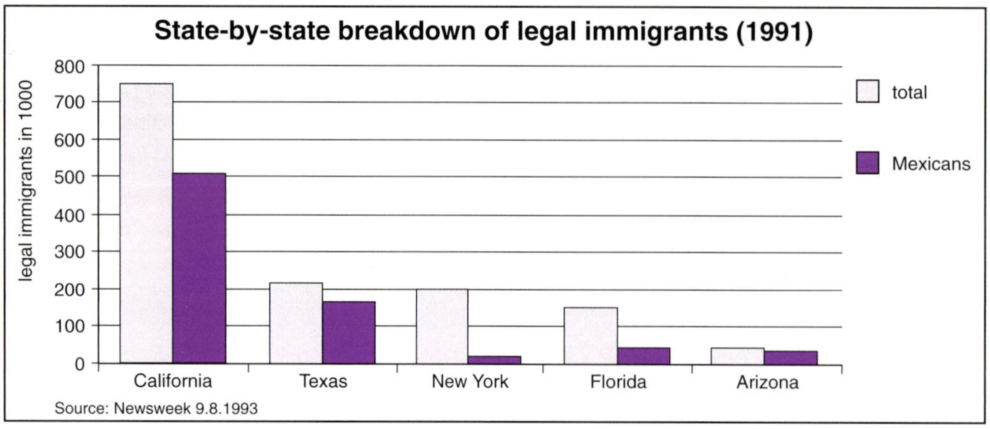

Chart 5

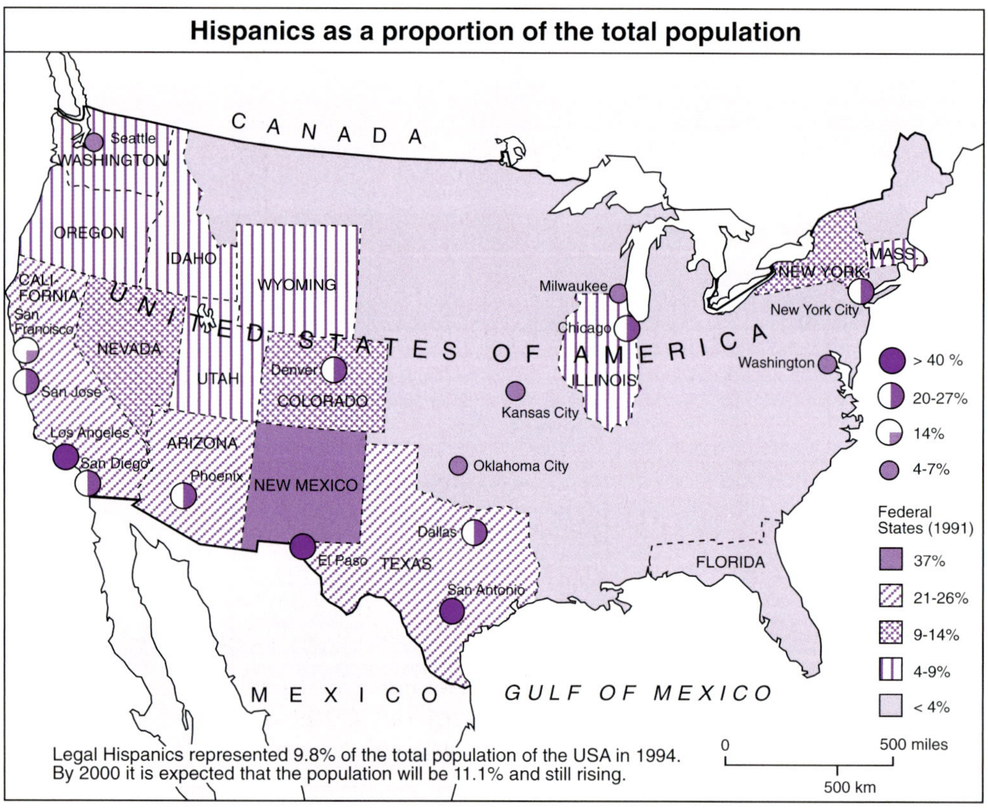

3. Comment on the proportion of Mexican immigrants in the states shown in charts 4 and 5.

Nach dem Vorlesen der Hausaufgabe werden die Schülerinnen und Schüler aufgefordert, in arbeitsteiliger Gruppenarbeit auf der Grundlage der Begegnung von Delaney und Jack Jardine im Supermarkt in Kapitel 7 deren unterschiedliche Positionen zur Einwanderungsproblematik herauszuarbeiten. Je eine Gruppe legt das Augenmerk auf Delaney bzw. Jack Jardine.

What are Delaney's and Jack's positions on immigration as voiced in their discussion in the supermarket? (Chapter I.7)

Es kann sich folgendes Tafelbild ergeben:

Delaney's versus Jack's position on immigration

Delaney
- gate irreconcilable with the foundations of democracy (p. 100)
- US has always been a nation of immigrants (p. 101)
- everyone deserves the chance to assimilate (p. 102)

Jack Jardine
- there must be a limit to the numbers of immigrants:
  a) immigration a question of national sovereignty (p. 101)
  b) US accepted more immigrants in one year than all the other countries of the world combined (p. 101)
  c) illegal immigrants are unskilled workers for whom demand is declining (p. 101)
  d) there are several categories of immigrants (p. 102)
  e) immigrants cost the taxpayer a lot for social services and they increase the crime rate (p. 102)

  ⇒ determination of violently defending his rights

Nachdem Delaney's liberale Einstellung zur Einwanderungsthematik im Gespräch mit Jack Jardine herauskristallisiert wurde, werden die Schüler mit der Frage konfrontiert, ob Delaney sich bei der tatsächlichen Begegnung mit Mexikanern so verhält, wie es seiner Haltung während der Diskussion entspricht. Auf der Grundlage von Kapitel 7 wird die folgende Fragestellung bearbeitet, deren Ergebnisse stichwortartig an der Tafel festgehalten werden können.

Comment on the conflict between Delaney's ideal of liberal humanism and his feelings and thoughts when confronted with Mexicans. (Chapter I.7)

Delaney's conflict

Delaney
- maintains a tolerant position on immigrants during the discussion with Jack Jardine (p. 100f.)

versus

- when meeting the Mexican again Delaney feels anger and shame, but does not offer to help him in any way (p. 105)
- in front of his computer Delaney is led into thinking that Cándido threw himself deliberately in front of his car in order to receive money (p. 109)
- seeing the Mexicans' camp he is filled with anger at people littering and intruding on the environment (p. 112) ⇒ desire to destroy the camp
- encountering the two Mexicans he wants to escape and have them taken back to their native country to stop them from producing more garbage (p. 117)
- after the car was stolen Delaney imagines Cándido behind the steering-wheel of his car (p. 120)

In der Hausaufgabe werden die Schüler und Schülerinnen aufgefordert, die während der Stunde gesammelten Aspekte bezüglich der Einstellungen von Delaney und Jack Jadine zur Einwanderungsthematik aufzuarbeiten:

Comment on the conflicting views of Delaney and Jack Jardine on Hispanic immigration.

Folgende Ausarbeitung könnte sich z. B. ergeben:

Delaney maintains the ideals of liberal humanism and is a passionate nature-lover. But when he hits the Mexican with his car, he is torn between conflicting feelings toward the man for the first time. On the one hand he is full of pity and sadness about the man's fate, on the other hand he loathes the pollution of the environment brought about by the illegal immigrants' camping and living out in the open. He still clings to the idealistic concept of America as a nation of immigrants and therefore vehemently objects to the construction of a gate in front of the property. In his eyes, the gate would exclude many people from the property which would put the residents in an élite-like position. Moreover, in the conversation with Jack Jardine in the supermarket he points out that every immigrant should have a chance to assimilate. When confronted with the Mexican for the second time, however, his former conflict of feelings arises again. Delaney represents the conflict between his beliefs in an ideal country of immigration and his emotional rejection of the people and circumstances related to the accident. Jack Jardine takes an unwavering position on the issue of immigration. Although a descendant of immigrants himself, he does not feel like an immigrant any more.
Apparently, for him there are several categories of immigrants. He feels justified in not wanting any more coming into the country and adds a number of reasons for his attitude. Among these is the fact that California is saturated with the huge numbers that have come in the past few years. Another reason is that the illegal immigrants constitute a large group of unskilled workers that are not needed so much any more. Additionally, the costs for the taxpayers in terms of social services and crime related expenses have soared.
Jack stands for the well-off upper-middle-class citizen who feels quite justified in his views and is afraid of being restricted in any way by growing numbers of immigrants. He is determined to use violence to defend his rights.

Component 2: Cándido's and América's Best of all Worlds

Zu Beginn sollten die Schülerinnen und Schüler aufgefordert werden, *Part Two* parallel zu der Arbeit an *Part One* zu lesen.

2.1 Symbolism

Boyle benutzt in *The Tortilla Curtain* auf verschiedenen Ebenen Symbole, um der Geschichte von Delaney und Cándido Nachdruck zu verleihen. Am auffälligsten dürften dabei die *telling names* sein, die sich in seinem Roman finden. Es ist daher nötig, die Schülerinnen und Schüler darauf aufmerksam zu machen, dass die Namen der Protagonisten nicht zufällig gewählt wurden.

Der Name der weißen Hauptpersonen, Delaney und Kyra Mossbacher, muss sicherlich erläutert werden. Boyle selbst definierte in einem Interview „Mossbacher" folgendermaßen: *"A mossback in the American language is someone who is a sort of stick-in-the-mud conservative who doesn't think for himself much ..."* (pointed out by Prof. Freese; can be found in: Erica Jong and T. Coraghessan Boyle, *Zwei Interviews*. Paderborn: Paderborner Universitätsreden 64, 1998, p. 24). Die Schülerinnen und Schüler sollten ausgehend von dieser Definition zu erklären versuchen, inwiefern dieser Name auf Delaney passt.

In view of Boyle's definition of a mossbach, why do you think he has chosen this name for Delaney?

Although Delaney calls himself a liberal humanist, it becomes clear that his liberalism is more of an attitude than a belief. He finds himself worrying about his car first and not the human victim of the accident, and it turns out that he can be influenced easily by his wife and friends.

Je nachdem wie weit die Schülerinnen und Schüler den Roman gelesen haben, kann sich eine Diskussion darüber entwickeln, ob Delaney wirklich liberal ist oder nicht. Im Verlauf der Besprechung des Romans wird dieser Aspekt immer wieder auftauchen.

Während Mossbach erläutert werden muss, können die Schülerinnen und Schüler sicherlich zu einigen anderen Namen im Roman Stellung nehmen. Dabei sollten Vermutungen über die Bedeutung von Cándidos Namen zurückgestellt werden.

What can you say about some of the other names in *Tortilla Curtain*?

América stands for both Americas, the southern part where a lot of poor people live and the northern part where these people desperately try to find a better life.
José Navidad, the rapist, stands for the Spanish conquerors who came to the America of the Indians and deprived them of everything they had, ironically his name means Christmas.
Jack **Cherrystone**, Doris **Obst** and Jack **Jardine** (jardin = garden in French) have names that refer to nature and gardens.
Also the fact that Jack Jardine's son has got the same name as his father suggests that there is not only a likeness in names, but that they have the same opinions and share the same political ideas.

Resurrección, Cándido's first wife, remains childless although her name suggests a renewing of life.

Beim weiteren Lesen sollten diese symbolischen Namen im Auge behalten werden. Wir lesen auf S. 204, dass América indianischer Abstammung ist, d. h. sie gehört zu den Ureinwohnern Amerikas (*"Indita. She hated it when he called her that: his little Indian"*). Ebenso treffen wir später auf Dominick Flood, der den Namen einer Naturgewalt trägt, was zu ihm passt, da er ein Verbrecher ist. Dies muss hier noch nicht erwähnt werden, da die Schülerinnen und Schüler ein *Worksheet* bekommen, auf dem sie laufend neue Erkenntnisse eintragen können.

Im weiteren Verlauf des Unterrichtsgesprächs können die Schülerinnen und Schüler dazu aufgefordert werden, Assoziationen zu „Cándido" zu äußern. Dabei könnten Latein-/Spanischschülerinnen und -schüler auf die Bedeutung *white* kommen, vom Autor wurde jedoch „Candide", der Held des gleichnamigen Romans von Voltaire, als Vorbild und Namensgeber seines Cándido genannt (pointed out bei Prof. Freese, in *Zwei Interviews*, p. 30). Vermutlich sind die Schülerinnen und Schüler diesem Roman noch nicht begegnet, daher bietet sich als Hausaufgabe an, sich über dieses Werk zu informieren. Dabei kann auf gängige Lexika, Literaturlexika, CD-ROMs (Grolier oder Bertelsmann) verwiesen werden. Falls eine Schulbücherei vorhanden ist, wird sich dort sicherlich eine Ausgabe Voltaires oder zumindest ein Literaturlexikon finden.

Find out what "Candide" by Voltaire is about and what kind of character Candide is. Explain why Cándido was named after him.

Candide is about a young man who sets out to find the best of all possible worlds. Voltaire wanted to refute Leibnitz' idea of a "best of all possible worlds" by writing this rather ridiculous account of his hero's pursuit of happiness. Candide meets all kinds of evil people and has to deal with numerous dangerous situations, he suffers all the bad luck possibly to be had, but still clings to his belief in the best of all worlds. The similarity between this 18th-century character and Boyle's Cándido is obvious. Where Candide is looking for the best of all worlds introduced to him by his philosophy teacher, Cándido is searching for happiness in the USA. Both encounter terrible situations and keep failing in the pursuit of success. However, Boyle's Cándido does not desire the best of all worlds, just a better life than the one he has in Mexico.

Bei der Namensgebung der Haustiere im Haushalt der Mossbachers erlaubt sich Boyle einen Scherz mit Kyra, die er hier als Intellektuelle darstellt, die ihren Hunden und ihrer Katze bedeutsame Namen gibt. Man kann die Enträtselung dieser Namen ebenfalls als Hausaufgabe geben, dann sollte man jedoch den Nachnamen von Dame Edith, Osbert und Sacheverell dazu nennen, nämlich Sitwell (pointed out by Prof. Freese). Wiederum sollten die Schülerinnen und Schüler aufgefordert werden, in Literaturlexika nachzuschlagen.

Find out who Dame Edith, Osbert and Sacheverell Sitwell were.

Dame Edith Sitwell (1887-1964) was a well-known poet, her younger brothers Osbert and Sacheverell were also known for their writings, Osbert as a poet, essayist and novelist and Sacheverell as an art historian. They constituted one of the most extraordinary literary families in the England of their time.

Als Hilfestellung für die Schülerinnen und Schüler kann man ihnen das folgende *Worksheet* austeilen, auf dem sie die Ergebnisse der Namensuntersuchungen eintragen können. Außerdem sollen sie aufgefordert werden, im Verlauf der Lektüre neue Erkenntnisse hinzuzufügen, z.B. über Américas Herkunft und über Dominick Flood.

Telling Names

Make notes to sum up your findings of the telling names in this novel and explain their function. Keep this list and add any new names or explanations.

Mossbacher: ______________________________

____

América: ______________________________

____

Cándido: ______________________________

____

José Navidad: ______________________________

____

Jack Jardine: ______________________________

____

Jack Cherrystone: ______________________________

____

Doris Obst: ______________________________

____

Dame Edith: ______________________________

____

Osbert: ______________________________

____

Sacheverell: ______________________________

____

Telling Names

Make notes to sum up your findings of the telling names in this novel and explain their function. Keep this list and add any new names or explanations.

Mossbacher:	mossback = conservative who does not think for himself Delaney is influenced easily
América:	stands for both Americas is the true America raped by Spanish conquerors
Cándido:	like Candide he is looking for a better life Boyle shows how futile this search is by giving him this name
José Navidad:	his name means Christmas which does not fit his very unattractive character
Jack Jardine:	his last name suggest a garden metaphor the fact that his son has the same name shows that they both share the same opinions
Jack Cherrystone:	his name also hints at gardening
Doris Obst:	her name also suggests gardens and nature all three represent the majority of white people who want to flee from big-city life, but are confronted with wildlife they cannot handle
Dame Edith:	poet (1887-1964)
Osbert:	younger brother of Edith, poet, essayist, novelist
Sacheverell:	art historian by naming her pets after the members of this literary family, Kyra is trying to be considered an intellectual

Nach Besprechung der Namen der Charaktere des Romans sollte man ebenso die Bezeichnung des Wohnkomplexes, in dem die Mossbachers leben, kurz untersuchen. Die Schülerinnen und Schüler sollten Seite 30 nochmals lesen.

Comment on the name and appearance of the Mossbacher's community, namely Arroyo Blanco, which is also the title of Part One.

Arroyo Blanco means white brook in Spanish. It is quite ironic that the expensive, exclusively white neighbourhood has got a Spanish name. Also the appearance of the homes is uniformly the same, they are all of Spanish Mission style, and even the colours are described with Spanish / Indian expressions ("Rancho White with Navajo trim", p. 30).
The aim of the Whites living in this Hispanic-looking area is to keep all minorities, especially the Hispanics, out of their premises.
By calling Part One Arroyo Blanco Boyle points out this irony from the start.

Nachdem im ersten Component die einzelnen Personen mit ihren unterschiedlichen Wünschen und Meinungen untersucht wurden, soll das Augenmerk der Schülerinnen und Schüler nun auf die Vergangenheit der Charaktere gelenkt werden. Dabei bieten sich América und Cándido an, da über die Vergangenheit der Mossbachers wenig berichtet wird. Vor der Besprechung sollte als Hausaufgabe *Chapter 4* nochmals gelesen worden sein.
Bei genauer Betrachtung von Cándidos Lebensgeschichte zeigen sich Parallelen zu alttestamentarischen Geschichten, auf die die Schülerinnen und Schüler in einem Unterrichtsgespräch vermutlich gestoßen werden müssen. Daher empfiehlt sich ein Tafelbild zur Zusammenfassung der Ergebnisse.

What do we learn about Cándido's and América's past? (Chapter 4)

p. 50	Cándido has known América since she was four he married her older sister Resurrección he worked in the north for nine months, was home for three, made a lot of money
p. 51	after seven years his wife left him for another man América brings him the bad news "Then came his season in hell" (l. 26)
p. 52	Cándido started drinking he met América again and changed still not as successful as before

Can you think of any stories that Cándido's life reminds you of?

There are two stories from the Bible mingled with this lifestory. On the one hand there is Joseph's story with seven good and seven bad years, on the other hand there is the story of his father Jacob who was tricked into first marrying Laban's older daughter Rachel and then her younger sister Leah.

Can you find other instances where Boyle refers to biblical scenes?

Delaney's stepson Jordan plays with his Nintendo and Delaney refers to the game as an "electronic Armageddon" (p. 103, l. 25f.) thus foreshadowing the real Armageddon that awaits the community.

Cándido compares himself to Job (p. 121), the classic case of someone enduring pain inflicted on him by God in order to test his faith (Book of Job, Old Testament). By saying that even Job would have broken down under these circumstances, Cándido admits that he is losing his faith in God.

Um auf weitere Symbole in diesem Roman hinzuweisen, sollten die Schülerinnen und Schüler nochmals die Szene laut lesen, in der Sacheverell von einem Kojoten gerissen wird (p. 36, l. 23: There was a silence ... – p. 40). Danach wird im Unterrichtsgespräch erörtert, ob es hierbei wirklich nur um Kojoten geht.

What does Sacheverell's capture stand for?

Sacheverell is called "The poor dog. It couldn't have defended itself from a rabbit." (p. 38) This shows that he has been changed by civilisation so much that he can no longer do what dogs are meant to do, e.g. chase rabbits. Wildlife in the form of a coyote, attracted by people in the first place, has taken his life without hesitation, taking what by natural law was its right to take.
Delaney himself has no chance of retrieving the dog. Since he has not got the ability to race a coyote, so the coyote proves to be the most reckless and fastest, leaving behind a terrified civilisation: "... mother and son, huddled in Jordan's narrow bed with Osbert and Dame Edith, looking like survivors of a shipwreck adrift on a raft." (p. 40)
So the human beings and their pets have tried to escape crime: "Crime? Up here? Wasn't that what they'd come here to escape?" (p. 43) to find that there are other dangers to be avoided: "... and there it was, wild nature ..." (p. 37).
When Cándido calls himself a "coyote" (p. 52) just a few pages later the reader can notice the parallels: Sacheverell stands for the whites and their lifestyle, the coyote stands for the poor Mexicans intruding and trying to participate in some of the whites' wealth.

Diese Parallele zwischen den Kojoten und den Mexikanern wird in dem Roman immer wieder aufgegriffen und sollte von den Schülerinnen und Schülern daher im Blick behalten werden. So wird der zweite Hund, Osbert, ebenfalls von einem Kojoten geholt, obwohl der Zaun inzwischen höher gemacht wurde, und Dame Edith wird von Cándido und América im dritten Teil verspeist.

Mexicans	**Coyotes**
live in canyon	live in canyon eat heartily among the rocks and the waste places (p. 79)
are believed to steal cars	hunting, gamboling, stealing (p. 76)
eat Dame Edith in Part Three (p. 322)	eat dogs (p. 36 and p. 194)

2.2 América – everybody's victim

Nach der Lektüre des ersten Teils ist den Schülerinnen und Schülern klar, dass die Mexikaner ihre Heimat verlassen und all die Strapazen auf sich nehmen, um ihren Traum vom besseren Leben in den USA zu verwirklichen. Um den Kontrast zwischen Traum und Wirklichkeit herauszustellen, sollten die Schülerinnen und Schüler nach erneuter häuslicher Lektüre des zweiten Kapitels die Lebensbedingungen von América und Cándido und ihren Traum beschreiben können. Die Ergebnisse dieser Hausaufgabe könnten in einem Tafelbild festgehalten werden.

Read chapter two again and describe in a few sentences the contrast between América's and Cándido's dreams and their living conditions.

Living conditions:
- they have a camp in a canyon by a streambed (p. 18)
- it is eight miles from this canyon to the labour exchange ⇒ work (p. 18)
- canyon is full of shrubs with thorns, snakes and spiders along the path to the highway (p. 19)
- they sleep on blankets in the sand (p. 24)
- they drink water from stream and have to make a fire every time they want to cook (p. 20)
- they move about in eternal fear of being stopped by the police (p. 19)
- after the accident Cándido cannot see a doctor despite his severe injuries; the only remedies they can afford are some food including meat, aspirin, alcohol and some Band-Aids (p. 21)

⇒ they live like fugitives under dreadful circumstances without any prospect of improvement

Dreams:
- América describes her dream herself: a house, a yard, maybe a TV and a car, too – nothing fancy, no palaces like the *gringos* built – just four walls and a roof (p. 29)

Die Realität für die Mexikaner wird jedoch immer bedrohlicher; am Ende von *Part One* wird América von einem Landsmann vergewaltigt. Diese Vergewaltigung kommt nicht als Überraschung für den Leser, da Boyle sie bereits vorbereitet hat. Die Schülerinnen und Schüler sollten in einer Gruppenarbeit herausfinden, inwiefern eine Atmosphäre der Bedrohung für América aufgebaut wurde. Die Ergebnisse können von den Schülerinnen und Schülern auf Folie festgehalten und anschließend bei ihrer Präsentation diskutiert werden.

América's rape has been foreshadowed. Find examples in the previous chapters.

- ... his wife, a barefoot girl from the country who didn't know a thing about the world, out there among all those men, those lowlifes who'd do anything for a buck – or a woman ... (p. 26)
- ... he'd warn América to douse the fire and keep out of sight (p. 27)
- Cándido remembers a twelve-year-old girl in Tijuana who was raped by a gang of men
- ... outlined the wickedness of the gabacho world and the perfidy of his fellow braceros at the labour exchange (p. 49)
- p. 58f.: The men were staring at her openly now, and their stares were harder, hungrier ...
- They were starving and she was fresh meat.
- ... looming nightmarishly, was the faces of those animals at the border – Mexican animals – the ones who'd come out of the night to attack her and Cándido as they crossed over.
- ... they went for her. A knife was in her face, their hands were all over her, and they jerked the clothes from her as if skinning a rabbit ...
- América meets the future rapist, he offers her coffee and she accepts. (p. 81)
- ... there was something rotten inside of him (p. 82)
- This was bad. This man was bad. ... she knew he was crazy, loco, demented ... (p. 83)
- And when the fat man laid his hand casually across her thigh, ... she wanted to fling it away from her ... She just let it lie there like a dead thing, though it moved and insinuated itself and she wanted to scream for the car to stop. (p. 97)

Nach dieser intensiven Beschäftigung mit América sollten die Schülerinnen und Schüler durch eine *creative writing*-Aufgabe dazu motiviert werden, in Américas Gemütszustand einzutauchen. Dabei eignet sich ein fiktiver Tagebucheintrag, allerdings ist von einem Eintrag am Tag der Vergewaltigung abzusehen. Es bietet sich an, América den ersten Arbeitstag und das darauf folgende Festmahl und ihre Gefühle während dieses Tages (Angst vor den Männern am *labour exchange* – Mary – die harte Arbeit – Ekel vor der Hand des Patron – Kaufrausch – romantische Situation mit Cándido) reflektieren zu lassen. Die Schülerinnen und Schüler sollten dafür nochmals Kapitel 6 und 8 bis S. 127 lesen.

C

Imagine América was able to write a diary. What would she write on the evening of her first workday? (Chapters 6 and 8 as far as p. 127)

Component 3: When Mexican Dreams Meet US Reality

3.1 Delaney's worries

In diesem *Component* werden Vorschläge zur Erarbeitung des zweiten Teils des Romans gemacht. Es werden dabei drei Hauptschwerpunkte gesetzt: zum einen eine Beschränkung auf die Entwicklung der weißen Protagonisten, dann eine genaue Betrachtung der Zwischenfälle, die Weiße und Mexikaner gleichermaßen betreffen, und im dritten Teil eine Bearbeitung der Textstellen, die sich ausschließlich auf die Mexikaner beziehen. Diese Unterteilung lässt den Lehrkräften Spielraum zum Setzen eigener Schwerpunkte. Es empfiehlt sich, eine Mischung aus jedem der drei Teile zu wählen. Alles ausführlich zu behandeln, wird aus Zeitgründen kaum machbar sein. Darüber hinaus erscheint es sinnvoll, die Kapitel 1, 2, 3 und 6 ausführlich zu behandeln.

Als Einstieg in diesen *Component* bieten sich verschiedene Wege an:

- Als die Leser das letzte Mal Delaney trafen, hatte er gerade festgestellt, dass sein Auto gestohlen wurde. Da Autodiebstahl auch in Deutschland ein viel diskutiertes Thema ist und auch hier bestimmte Gruppen, vor allem polnische und andere osteuropäische Bürger, unter Vorverurteilung leiden, bietet sich ein Einstiegsgespräch über das Thema im Vergleich Deutschland – Kalifornien an.
- Der Arbeitsauftrag *What do you know about Thanksgiving?* könnte im Sinne eines *Brainstorming* ebenfalls an den Anfang dieses *Component* gestellt werden. Die Schülerinnen und Schüler könnten so ihre Kenntnisse über diesen Feiertag und seinen Ursprung präsentieren *(Fourth Thursday of November, started in 1621 by William Bradford, who wanted to thank God for helping the settlers in their first difficult years in the new world. The settlers shared their food with the American Indians who had helped them to survive.)* Anschließend sollte eine Diskussion zum Titel des 2. Teils *El Tenksgeevee* erfolgen: *Comment on what this title means for the characters of this novel. In which way and for whom can a Thanksgiving be expected? (Cándido and América could be thankful for having made it to the US, they could be looking forward to their baby and the apartment they are saving all their money for. Delaney and Kyra could be thankful for their nice home in Arroyo Blanco, Kyra could go on doing good business with newly built homes in the suburbs of Los Angeles. Delaney could be thankful for living close to nature and being able to write his reports.)*

Nach einem solchen Einstiegsgespräch kann mit der direkten Arbeit am Text begonnen werden. Dabei sollte Delaneys Reaktion auf den Autodiebstahl und das Desinteresse seiner Umwelt zuerst behandelt werden. Kenny Grissoms Meinung zu den illegalen Einwanderern unterscheidet sich nicht wesentlich von Jack Jardines Ansichten; eine genauere Betrachtung des Autohändlers bietet sich an, da Delaney durch ihn in der Veränderung seiner Haltung gegenüber Einwanderern beeinflusst wird.

What effect does the theft of his car have on Delaney? How do others react to the crime? (Chapter 1)

Delaney is disappointed because everybody seems to calmly accept the fact that someone stole his car. The fact that many cars are stolen is no comfort to him. The frequent repetition of the phrase "happens all the time" (four times in the first three paragraphs of this chapter) and the police's "enthusiasm of the walking dead" (p. 146) when taking the report demonstrate just how very normal an incident like this is. It is regarded as inevitable as "tax, winter floods and mudslides" (p. 146) (The mentioning of "mudslide" here is also a foreshadowing of the end of the novel.) Kenny Grissom's remark that he does not blame it all on the Mexicans, but also on "Salvadorians, Iranians, Russians, Vietnamese" (p. 147) shows that he does not think at all that a white American could possibly have stolen the car. In this respect he is just as racist in his attitude as Jack Jardine who uses this crime to influence Delaney further and to change his attitude from sympathetic to racist. He calls people like Delaney "bleeding hearts" (p. 146) who invite all the world to come to the USA. He compares the situation in Arroyo Blanco with a war: "We're under siege here – and there's going to be a blacklash" (p. 146). (The backlash possibly being a foreshadowing of the scene where Delaney and his upper-middle-class neighbours turn into a nasty mob (p. 286ff.)).
A first consequence of all this talk is that Delaney feels somewhat reluctant to hand his new car over to the young Hispanic who is the valet parking attendant of the Indian restaurant where he wants to meet Kyra for lunch.

What can you say about Kenny Grissom's views on Mexicans / illegal immigrants? (Chapter 1)

- seems to be happy about many car thefts – good for business
- knows a lot about exact proceedings of these thefts (who orders, who sells ...)
- makes fun of ignorant woman from Guatemala

⇒ typical car dealer, viewing everything from the businessman's point of view

Why does Delaney have the feeling of "losing control" (p. 148) and "as if his luck had turned bad" (p. 149)?

Delaney's comfortable life has been disturbed by his inner conflict about how to feel about the Mexicans. Also the tragic losses of Sacheverell and his car have shaken him. It seems as if the American way is no longer working for him. "Buy something. Feel good. But he didn't feel good, not at all. He felt like a victim." (p. 149) Of course, he is a victim, after all his car has been stolen.
An example of his loss of control is that he cannot remember his new license plate number. He used to have personalised number plates, namely PILGRIM, and the fact that he does without these shows that he has already given up some of his identity as Pilgrim to Topanga Creek, living in harmony with society and nature.

Ein Ziel bei der Bearbeitung eines Romans ist die stilistische Analyse von Textstellen. Um den Schülerinnen und Schülern dabei Hilfestellungen zu geben, findet sich hier ein zweiseitiges Worksheet mit den in *Tortilla Curtain* häufig vorkommenden stilistischen Mitteln. Die ausgewählte Textstelle, *Part Two, Chapter 1* bietet sich besonders für ein solches Unterfangen an, da T. C. Boyle hier konzentriert Stilmittel einsetzt, um dem Leser Delaneys sich allmählich wandelnde Einstellung deutlich zu machen. Dabei werden sowohl komische als auch ernsthafte Effekte erzielt. Man sollte zunächst gemeinsam mit den Schülerinnen und Schülern die aufgelisteten Stilmittel besprechen, sie im Textzusammenhang nachlesen und ihren jeweiligen Effekt untersuchen. Daraufhin können die beiden *Assignments* entweder als Partnerarbeit oder als Hausaufgabe gestellt werden.

Stylistic Devices

This is a list of stylistic devices that T. C. Boyle uses quite frequently in *The Tortilla Curtain:*

1) **anaphora**
A word or phrase is repeated at the beginning of each of two or more successive clauses, sentences or paragraphs.
p. 146: "Jack, ever calm, ever prepared, ever cynical ..."

2) **alliteration**
Repetition of similar sounds in a sequence of associated words.
p. 147: "... story of the woman who'd wrecked ..."

3) **climactic sentence structure**
A series of words or ideas in an ascending order of significance or intensity.
p. 149: "... he felt good about it, good about himself, the future of the country, the state of the world."

4) **exaggeration**
An exaggeration makes s.th. seem more important, better or worse than it is.
p. 146: "when all you bleeding hearts want to invite the whole world in here."

5) **flashback**
Interruption of the account of sth in order to portray an incident or a scene from the past.
pp. 167-174: Cándido thinks about his first stay in the canyon six years ago.

6) **interior monologue**
Author's technique that reproduces the flow of thoughts just as it occurs in a character's mind.
p. 156: Kyra on her way to an appointment.

7) **irony**
Humorous use of words to express a meaning other than the one literally conveyed by the words.
p. 147: story about the woman from Guatemala who took the advertisement "we don't refuse credit" too literally.

8) **metaphor**
The transference of a term from the object it ordinarily designates to an object it may designate only by implicit comparison or analogy.
p. 145f.: Slim Jim as a name for breaking into cars.

9) **paratactical sentence structure**
The joining together of clauses without the use of conjunctions.
p. 147: "And now Kenny Grissom. Business as usual. A shoulder shrug, a wink of commiseration, the naked joy of moving product."

10) **rhetorical question**
A question to which no answer is expected.
p. 146: "Where do you think they sleep? What do you think they eat?"

11) **sarcasm**
Apparent praise for dispraise.
p. 146: "... enthusiasm of the walking dead."

12) **simile**
Two unlike things are compared, indicated by a marker such as "like" or "as".
p. 146: "It was <u>like</u> a tax, <u>like</u> winter floods and mudslides."

Read closely Part Two, Chapter 2, p. 171 ("And then the roof fell in ...") to p. 174 ("... and went home to Resurrección"). Find as many stylistic devices as you can and explain the intended effect.

Hier ein kurzer Erwartungshorizont für die Aufgabe auf *Worksheet 6*:

anaphora
p. 173 "Was it worth dying for this? ... It wasn't worth it. ... It wasn't worth it."
p. 174 "He watched the trees ... He watched the groundsquirrels, the birds, watched light ..."

alliteration
p. 171 "... poor possessions ..."
p. 172 "... Spanish speaking Immigration ..."
"... acquiesce, accept."
p. 173 "... ragged roaring ..."

climactic sentence structure
p. 171 "... the doors locked, the windows barred, all their possessions – ... – left behind."

exaggeration
p. 173 "... then the sound of all the glass in the world shattering."

flashback
die gesamte Szene ist Teil eines Flashbacks.

Interior monologue
p. 172 "Run! Run now while ..."

metaphor
p. 171 "... puke-green buses ..."
p. 172 "... and the Mexicans ... rooted to the pavement ..."
"... the torrent of headlights."
p. 173 "... ragged roaring whine of engines ..."
"... sirens tore at the air ..."
"... while the apocalypse of twisted metal and skating cars blasted the world around him till even the traffic across the divider was stopped dead in horror."
"... walked ... on melting legs ..."

paratactical sentence structure
p. 172 "It was cold. A woman was crying softly beside him; a man argued with ..."

rhetorical question
p. 173 "Was it worth dying for this?"

simile
p. 173 "The first boy went down like a piston ..."

An dieser Stelle kann man problemlos in den zweiten Teil dieses *Components* einsteigen und dort die erste Teilfrage bearbeiten. Man kann aber auch weiterhin konzentriert auf Delaney die Arbeit fortsetzen und einen Stillleseauftrag kombiniert mit der nachfolgenden Aufgabe für eine Partner- bzw. Gruppenarbeit stellen. Als Hausaufgabe bietet sich dann eine Bearbeitung der letzten Frage dieses Teils des *Components* an.

Demonstrate the symbolism of Chapter 5 taking into consideration Sacheverell's capture in Chapter 3 (p. 37 – p. 39).

T. C. Boyle wants to draw a comparison between the coyotes and the Mexicans who also "keep coming, breeding up to fill in the gaps, moving in where the living is easy. They are cunning, versatile, hungry and unstoppable" (p. 215). It is possible that Delaney at this point in the novel has not even made that comparison consciously. With reference to Sacheverell's capture, it can be said that although Kyra had the fence put up higher, a coyote succeeds in capturing Osbert later on. Similarly, the inhabitants of Arroyo Blanco try to protect themselves against crime, mainly committed by Mexicans, by putting a wall around their community. So the coyotes again stand for the Mexicans and Sacheverell / Osbert stand for the community.

Work out the development of Delaney's position towards the building of a wall and the presence of illegal immigrants in Chapter 6.

- vehement opposition "But that's crazy" (p. 219)
- clear anti-racist attitude in discussion (p. 220)
- tolerance towards Mexicans
- worried about Jordan's future in Arroyo Blanco
- doubts about his own attitudes "... his mind gone numb with ambivalence." (p. 227)
- clear racist behaviour when personally confronted with Mexican (pp. 228/229)

Nach der Erarbeitung dieses Schwerpunktes kann jetzt am nächsten Aspekt, dem Zusammentreffen von Weißen und Mexikanern, weitergearbeitet werden.

3.2 When Whites and Mexicans meet

Die folgende Aufgabe eignet sich zur Bearbeitung in Partnerarbeit, die Ergebnisse können stichwortartig an der Tafel festgehalten werden.

How do the Mossbachers establish contact with the Mexicans in Chapter 1?

- There is indirect contact when Kenny Grissom tells Delaney that rich Mexicans order cars to be stolen by their countrymen in California (pp. 145-147).
- Delaney hands his new car to the parking valet who is a Latino, Delaney feels a moment of racist resentment at that encounter (p. 149).
- The fear of another Mexican gang stealing his new car makes Delaney sit in the bushes, not daring to leave his car alone in the wilderness, watching it instead of going on a hike (p. 155f.).
- Kyra becomes aware of how many Mexicans are hanging around Ventura Boulevard just a couple of blocks away from her business area and she decides to do something about it (p. 158f.). Ironically, the Mexicans were at first good for her business because they made rich white people want to leave Los Angeles' inner city areas.
- When Kyra stops to buy something at a small supermarket she feels all the Mexican men's eyes on her, a young man offers himself as a cheap worker to her (p. 158f.).

- Kyra decides to have a higher fence because of what has happened to Sacheverell; when she watches the Mexicans who work for her contractor, Al Lopez (obviously also an immigrant from south of the border), she recognises Cándido as the man who was hit by Delaney's car (p. 161).
- Later, when she is closing down the Da Ros place she notices a shopping cart in the bush; she checks the area and meets two Mexicans, who should not be there. It seems as if they are the same men who raped América earlier. Kyra is afraid of them, but manages to scare them away (pp. 161-165).

Nachdem die Schülerinnen und Schüler die Beziehungen von Weißen und Mexikanern zu Beginn des zweiten Teils untersucht haben, können sie nun detailliert auf die unterschiedlichen Frauenrollen in den beiden Kulturen anhand von América und Kyra eingehen.

América and Kyra represent two totally different types of women. Comment on the two different roles as women that América and Kyra assume.

América	**Kyra**
in eternal fear of being caught by La Migra, sometimes hit and abused by husband (p. 182)	assertive, courageous businesswoman, violently confronts a man who does not treat his pet correctly in her opinion (p. 150)
not daring to defend herself when sexually abused (grabs, rape) (p. 97)	when passing a group of Mexicans she is in control (p. 158)
feels uneasy and menaced when she is near Mexican men (p. 82)	although fearful she confronts the two trespassers (p. 165)
⇒ submissive, fearful and completely subject to her husband's will	⇒ self-assertive, independent woman fighting for her rights

Ein weiterer interessanter Aspekt dieses *Parts* ist das Verhältnis der illegalen Einwanderer zu *La Migra*, der Einwanderungsbehörde. Nach dem Vorlesen der Seiten 171-173 können die Schülerinnen und Schüler in Partnerarbeit und im anschließenden Unterrichtsgespräch untersuchen, wie T. C. Boyle sprachlich Cándidos Verachtung für Angehörige dieser Behörde zum Ausdruck bringt, obwohl ein eigentlicher Grund zum Hass nicht gegeben ist. Die Vermutung liegt nahe, dass er seine eigenen Schuldgefühle durch Hass auf *La Migra* betäuben möchte.

How does Cándido describe members of La Migra? (Chapter 2)

The overall impression of the Border Patrol tends to be very negative. The reader sees the immigration officers only through the eyes of this illegal immigrant whose one and only concern is how to get past them. He uses derogatory language:
- puke-green buses (p. 171)
- fat-faced overfed pendejo (p. 172)

- green-eyed bitch (p. 172)
- macho corps of the immigration (p. 172)
- their faces contorted and ugly with their shouts and threats (p. 173)

Cándido seems to hate La Migra so much that even faced by the greatest danger, he does not want to give himself up to them. "Something uncoiled inside of him ... like a cornered rabbit leaping from a cliff to avoid the dogs." (p. 173) Nevertheless, he knows all the time that nothing worse will happen than being sent home and having to return a couple of days later.

How do the immigration agents treat the illegal immigrants they catch? (Chapter 2)

Cándido's own knowledge of what is likely to happen if they get arrested by the Border Patrol belies his negative utterances. While in some countries they would face severe beatings, could be killed or sentenced to many years in detention camps or prisons, the American immigration agents will merely transport them back to or beyond the border (p. 173). From there, the Mexicans can attempt any number of new crossings until they succeed.

What makes Cándido feel that he "would never forgive himself for what happened next"? (Chapter 2, p. 173)

Reflecting on the fatal accidents, he is aware that only he knew the real risks that the whole situation along the freeway posed. He thinks he should have known that the freeway was much more dangerous than the immigration agents behind them. Running across the freeway meant risking their lives, but being picked up by La Migra only meant that they could be back "in a day ... a week" (p. 173).
It was also his responsibility to take care of the two young men not only because of his age, but also because of his greater experience on North American soil. He should have put the welfare of the group above his own. His hate of La Migra was so strong that he followed his self-destructive impulse, "something uncoiled inside of him" (p. 173).

Nach Abschluss der intensiven Besprechung dieser Episode bietet sich eine *creative writing*-Aufgabe als Hausaufgabe an. Dabei sollen die Schülerinnen und Schüler darauf achten, die Fakten richtig wiederzugeben und eine eigene Stellungnahme bzw. eigene Gefühle mit einzubringen.

C

You are a reporter for an American newspaper. By chance, you have seen the two attempts made by Cándido and his two companions at escaping the immigration officers. Write an article about what you have witnessed.
OR:
You are one of the officers involved in this incident. At the police station you tell your colleagues about it.

Als Alternative bietet sich eine Übung im Schreiben von *comments* an. Wiederum gibt es die Möglichkeit, unter zwei Themen zu wählen.

In 1994 a high fence was added to the central divide between the northbound and southbound lanes of the San Diego Freeway as one approaches the INS (Immigration and Naturalization Service) checkpoint at San Onofre from the south. What does this development tell you about the immigration situation in Southern California?

OR:
It is estimated that three to four million illegal immigrants currently live in California. About 300,000 to 500,000 are believed to cross the 2,500 mile US-Mexican border every year. How are these figures likely to influence readers' views of Cándido's escape? (Personal comment)

Selbstverständlich eignen sich diese Aufgaben auch hervorragend für Klausuren. In der folgenden Stunde werden die Ergebnisse der Hausaufgabe besprochen. Die Schüler können jetzt die im Kapitel 2 geschilderten geographischen Gegebenheiten visuell umsetzen, indem sie ein großformatiges Bild erstellen. Ein gelungenes Bild wird dann gemeinsam ausgesucht und der Romancollage hinzugefügt (vgl. *Component 2*).

In Kapitel 3 kommt es erneut zu einem Treffen einiger Mitglieder der *Arroyo Blanco community*. Die Seiten 188-192 sollten die Schülerinnen und Schüler laut mit verteilten Rollen lesen, danach kann mit der arbeitsteiligen Gruppenarbeit begonnen werden, bei der einzelne Positionen herausgearbeitet werden. Nach Erstellen des Tafelbildes wird eine Diskussion in der Klasse geführt.

At the community's second meeting various opinions are voiced by the inhabitants. Identify the speakers and their statements, then have a similar discussion in class. (Chapter 3)
For your own discussion think of liberal arguments that Delaney might have had at the beginning of this novel and have one group be a supporter of such liberal humanist ideas.

Jim Shirley
- suggests that phone numbers should not be listed any more, he gives two examples of tricks that are used by Mexican burglars

⇒ introduction of more security measures

- dwells on the details of a particularly heavy assault on a resident

⇒ purpose of shocking the listeners and getting their support for more security

Jack Jardine
- suggests that the area should be walled in by pointing out the weaknesses of a gate

⇒ introduction of even stronger security measures

Dominick Flood
- reports that the labour exchange will be closed down because of his intervention

⇒ emphasis on strong measures to drive Mexicans away

Jack Cherrystone
- project of labour exchange was wrong from the start
- high unemployment rate in Los Angeles
- a future reduction in the crime rate
- too many Mexicans everywhere

⇒ emphasis on strong measures to drive Mexicans away

Work out the differences between the first (p. 39f.) and the second (pp. 187ff.) community meeting.

Whereas in the first meeting some residents still point out the freedom of every individual and resent any kind of elitist behaviour or discrimination of some groups, the anti-Mexican tendency is voiced much more strongly and the measures to be taken are much more vehement in the second meeting. Nobody mentions the desperate situation of the Mexicans. It is interesting to note that the person who finally takes the decisive steps in uprooting the labour exchange is somebody who has been sentenced himself. His offence was mishandling funds, in other words he is a thief, even though he seems to be socially accepted. At the second meeting Delaney does not make any comment except an irritated remark in which he anticipates the plan that they all have: a wall around the estate. Having been confronted with it, Delaney is silent. There is only one other occasion when he says something, that is when the others slightly make fun of him because of his appearance during the last meeting when speaking out against feeding the wildlife.
Summing up, the tone of the second meeting is much more aggressive and assertive than that of the first one. The issue is only looked at from one side except for Delaney's little outburst.

Entweder als Hausaufgabe oder als Stillarbeit in der Klasse bietet sich eine Leseaufgabe zu Kapitel 8 an, deren Ergebnis kurz als Tafelbild festgehalten werden kann. Auch könnte man das Interesse der Schülerinnen und Schüler auf Kyra lenken, die hier kurz charakterisiert wird.

Show how the mood of the two couples is influenced by the exposure to special foods.

Delaney and Kyra	**Cándido and América**
they have an argument about the necessity of the wall and the responsibility of the Da Ros place	América suffers from a nervous breakdown and is completely shattered
the superabundant variety of the goods in the supermarket makes Delaney feel tender towards Kyra	The free gift of the turkey raises Cándido's spirits enormously and the prospect of eating improves América's mental state
⇒ they are reconciled	⇒ she smiles again

We witness the giving away of two turkeys at the supermarket. What are the differences? (Chapter 8)

When Kyra and Delaney get their turkey, a new trait of Kyra's is revealed. She is greedy for the turkey although the Mossbachers have already got one. She cuts Delaney short when he starts to refuse the gift. By doing that she confirms Cándido's prejudice about the greedy whites who, although living in the best circumstances, still want more and more.

When Cándido is offered the turkey by the two men who are in line in front of him, he does not even realize what they are doing. He is really thankful and feels very lucky for a change.

3.3 The Mexicans' desperate struggle for happiness

Im dritten Teil dieses *Components* finden sich Anregungen zur Diskussion von Problemen, die die Lebensumstände von Cándido und América betreffen. Als Einstieg in ein Unterrichtsgespräch über deren Situation könnte die Frage dienen, ob die Schülerinnen und Schüler sich in ihre Lage versetzen können. Obwohl dies vermutlich verneint werden muss, können in einem Tafelbild stichwortartig einzelne Lebensbedingungen, die in *Part One* beschrieben wurden, festgehalten werden. Es darf spekuliert werden, wie sich die Lebensverhältnisse der beiden weiter entwickeln könnten (vgl. Diskussion zum Titel von *Part Two, El Tenksgeevee*).

Falls bereits über die unterschiedlichen Rollen von Frauen in diesem Roman gesprochen wurde, erübrigt sich ggf. die nachfolgende Frage, falls nicht, ergibt sich aus dieser Frage vermutlich ein lebhaftes Gespräch über Frauenrollen, bzw. Gewalt in der Familie.

Why does Cándido hit his wife (Chapter 2)?

He hits América because she is the person in his life who is even weaker and less successful than he is. He must find a way of relief for his frustration and wants to feel superior to someone.

Bezugnehmend auf die Bearbeitung wesentlicher Fragen des vorangegangenen Teils kann hier noch einmal auf die dort erarbeiteten Ergebnisse zurückgegriffen werden und Cándidos und Américas unterschiedliche Reaktionen auf die Nachricht, dass der *Labour Exchange* geschlossen wurde, untersucht werden. Es bietet sich hier eine kleine Gruppenarbeit an; eine Gruppe untersucht Cándidos Reaktion, eine andere Américas. In der anschließenden Diskussion wird ein Tafelbild erstellt.
Die beiden jetzt folgenden Aufgaben bieten sich auch als Klausuraufgaben an. Falls die stilistischen Mittel in den vorhergehenden Aufgaben besprochen wurden, kann auch noch die anschließende Arbeitsanweisung als Klausuraufgabe herangezogen werden.

Why is Cándido so shocked when he finds out that the labour exchange is closed? (Chapter 4)

Cándido is shocked because he wants to protect América from the dangerous life in the street. He has planned to save all the money they need and then move to an apartment directly from the canyon. He knows life in the cities from his previous stays in the US.
He feels that they have been quite close to success and is angry that now they will have to leave the canyon. He momentarily thinks of committing suicide: "Why not kill himself now and get it all over with?" (p. 199) and "Or should he just die on the spot ..." (p. 201). He compares Mexico, the country to which he cannot return, to the USA where obviously he cannot survive either. He is mad about the fact that he is refused the right to work.

Why is América quite happy when she hears the news? (Chapter 4)

América is bored by her dull life alone in the canyon. She also wants to have a bath and a bed since she is troubled by her pregnancy. She is afraid of the people in the canyon and she is constantly reminded of the rape. She dreams of a much better life in the city.

Read pp. 199–200 again and compare the information given about Mexico and the USA.

Mexico

- 40% unemployment
- 1 million people a year entering the work force
- only rich people enough to eat
- people living in extreme poverty

USA

- right to riches of the world
- white faces, high heels, business suits, greedy eyes, ravenous mouths
- glass palaces
- the value of exercise equipment alone is enough to feed a Third World country
- even the poorest have got two cars

Sum up the incidents that lead to América's and Cándido's further defeat and their reactions to them. Then try to identify some of the stylistic devices T. C. Boyle uses to emphasise their desperate situation.

1. Several hours América waits for Cándido to come back. However, he does not show up.
   ⇒ she is worried and approached by insinuating men (p. 232)
2. Cándido tells her that he has been robbed.
   ⇒ all their hopes for the future are shattered (p. 230)
3. Cándido rummages in the trash to find something to eat.
   ⇒ América is completely disgusted and refuses to take anything (p. 238f.)

ad 1)
América's anxiety is reflected by the many questions which she is asking herself:
"... and where was he?" (p. 231)
"... what if he'd had an accident? What if he was hurt? What if La Migra had snatched him? ... What if Cándido never came back, what if he'd died of a heart attack or got hit by another car? What then?" (p. 232)
"And where was Cándido? Where was the room he'd promised her, the bed, the shower?" (p. 233)

This stylistic device of repeated questions emphasises América's fear and insecurity. She is, after all, a girl who is very young and inexperienced.

ad 2) and 3)
Metaphors and similes are used to show their defeat:
"... his face a flag of blood, his pantlegs flapping like ragged banners" (p. 236)
"... his shoulders squared up like a fighting cock's, his eyes eating up the street" (p. 236)

⇒ He is compared to a fighting cock that cannot decide for himself but is pulled by invisible strings. He has to fight to survive, he is also ravenously hungry.

"... like a hermit crab emerging from its shell" (p. 238)

⇒ In the same way as the only possession of the hermit crab is the shell, Cándido's only access to survival or food is the trash bin.

Um die Schülerinnen und Schüler auch emotional an die Problematik heranzuführen, kann man eine Diskussion zum Thema Eigenverantwortung mit ihnen über die nächste Frage anregen. Dabei könnten eigene Erfahrungen der Schülerinnen und Schüler mit eingebracht werden.

Cándido thinks that again his "stinking bad luck" (p. 235) has struck. Do you agree? (Chapter 7)

There are two ways of seeing this: either the students agree that it is just his tough luck or they find arguments for Cándido's own fault in his predicament, e.g. how could he have brought a young girl to the US, why is he so stupid and careless? They could report personal experiences with situations where they thought it was their tough luck that foiled their success or on the other hand situations where they realized that they had made mistakes.

Da die Frage des *point of view* bereits in *Component 1, Worksheet 2* behandelt wurde, bietet es sich an, eine erneute Aufgabe zu dem Thema zu stellen, um den Schülerinnen und Schülern anhand eines weiteren Beispiels deutlich zu machen, dass der *point of view* einen beträchtlichen Einfluss auf den Stil und die Wirkung eines Romans hat. Am Beispiel des Kapitels 6 kann man besonders gut zeigen, wie die Erzählperspektive die Emotionen der Leser wecken und ein direktes Mitfühlen mit den Protagonisten ermöglichen kann.

Chapter 7 is mainly told from América's point of view, Cándido's thoughts are only presented to a very limited extent. What effect does this have on the reader?

The reader is told a lot about América's anxiety while waiting for Cándido as well as about her feelings about being in the US in general: "You got streets and bums and burning pee." (p. 233)
América's reaction to the news of having lost everything comes out very clearly; her shattered hopes are voiced and she even wants to die.
When Cándido rummages in the trash América's complete horror and outrage is voiced, she even points to the greater respectability of her family than Cándido's in her despair (p. 238). This is also a scene where T.C. Boyle shows his talent for irony. If the perspective was on Cándido, América's reactions and thoughts could never have been presented to the reader so clearly. Her disgust, outrage and despair become apparent and genuine.

Write down an interior monologue (see: Worksheet Stylistic Devices) for Cándido on his way back to América after having been mugged.

Falls man nicht allzu ausführlich auf die vorherigen Fragen eingehen möchte, bietet sich als Abschluss der Bearbeitung des zweiten Teils eine Rückschau auf die Träume der beiden und ihre reale Situation an.

What are the Mexicans' dreams and which nightmares do they have to endure?

dreams	**nightmares**
car, apartment (p. 181)	money stolen / América suffers as a result of rape
América dreams of city with shops, toilets, showers (p. 202)	dog-eat-dog world (p. 180)
motel room for one night with shower and TV (p. 203)	no work for Cándido because illegal immigrant
América falls into trance when she is looking at a furniture store (p. 207)	they eat little birds (p. 197)
regular work with Señor Willis (p. 251)	closing down of labour exchange live on streets temptation to steal, humiliation at being given alms (p. 201f.) realisation: no work in the city (p. 209) Cándido ripped off in the city (p. 234) eating from trash cans (p. 238) canyon on fire (p. 257)

Notizen:

Component 4:
Delaney – Racist in a Liberal Skin

4.1 The wound refusing to heal

Der vierte und letzte *Component* geht auf den gesamten Roman ein, insbesondere jedoch den II. und III. Teil. Das Hauptaugenmerk liegt auf der Figur des Delaney, dessen allmähliche Wandlung vom liberalen Humanisten zum aggressiven Rassisten, hervorgerufen durch die Veränderungen in seiner Umgebung, herausgearbeitet wird. Voraussetzung für die Behandlung dieses *Component* ist, dass der gesamte Roman gelesen wurde, die Kapitel I.1, I.3. I.7, II.1, II.3, II.5, II.6, III.3, III.5, III.7 und III.8 intensiv, die restlichen extensiv.
Als Einstieg in den *Component* bietet es sich an, auf der Grundlage der *„1994 California Voter Information: Proposition 187, Text of Proposed Law“* den Schülerinnen und Schülern *Worksheet 7* vorzulegen. In diesem *Worksheet* sind die wichtigsten Aussagen von *Proposition 187* zusammengestellt und darüber hinaus Argumente dafür und dagegen aufgelistet. Diese können durch Schülerbeiträge noch ergänzt werden. Das *Worksheet* kann als Grundlage für eine Diskussion über die Einwandererpolitik in den USA dienen.
Im November 1994 stimmten die Kalifornier mit einer Mehrheit von 59 % für *Proposition 187*. Nachdem sie dem Bund zur Abstimmung vorgelegt worden war, wurde sie jedoch von Washington zurückgewiesen.

Read the following worksheet and discuss the present immigration policy in the United States, considering the arguments in favour and against Proposition 187 as stated in this worksheet.

Notizen:

Proposition 187: Main statements – excerpts

1. The People of California find and declare as follows:

   a) That they have suffered and are suffering economic hardship caused by the presence of illegal aliens in this state.
   b) That they have suffered and are suffering personal injury and damage caused by the criminal conduct of illegal aliens in this state.
   c) That they have a right to the protection of their government from any person or persons entering this country unlawfully.
   d) Therefore, the People of California declare their intention to provide for cooperation between their agencies of state and local government with the federal government, and to establish a system of required notification, by and between such agencies to prevent illegal aliens in the United States from receiving benefits or public services in the state of California.

2. Every law enforcement agency in California shall fully cooperate with the United States Immigration and Naturalization Service regarding any person who is arrested if he or she is suspected of being present in the United States in violation of federal immigration laws.

3. In order to carry out the intention of the People of California that only citizens of the United States and aliens lawfully admitted to the United States may receive the benefits of public social services and to ensure that all persons employed in the providing of those services shall diligently protect public funds from misuse, the provisions of this section are adopted.

4. In order to carry out the intention of the People of California that, excepting emergency medical care as required by federal law, only citizens of the United States and aliens lawfully admitted to the United States may receive the benefits of publicly-funded health care, and to ensure that all persons employed in the providing of those services shall diligently protect public funds from misuse, the provisions of this section are adopted.

5. No public elementary or secondary school shall admit, or permit the attendance of and no public institution of post secondary education shall admit, enroll, or permit the attendance of any person who is not a citizen of the United States, an alien lawfully admitted as a permanent resident in the United States, or a person who is otherwise authorized under federal law to be present in the United States.

(1994 California Voter Information: Proposition 187, Text of Proposed Law)

Lösungsvorschlag zu Worksheet 1

Arguments in favour of Proposition 187

1. California can strike a blow for the taxpaper that will be heard across America; in Arizona, in Texas, in Florida in the same way Proposition 13 was heard across the land.
2. It has been estimated that illegal aliens are costing taxpayers an excess of 5 billion dollars a year.
3. Illegal aliens receive taxpayer – subsidized education including college.
4. Classrooms are overcrowded with illegal children.
5. Illegal aliens are able to buy and sell forged documents without penalty.
6. The State Legislature voted on July 5th to remove dental care as a medical option and force the increase of the cost of prescription drugs for Senior Citizens. On the other hand, they voted to continue free pre-natal care for illegal aliens.

Arguments against Proposition 187

1. Proposition 187 does not do a thing to beef up the enforcement at the border. It does not even crack down on employers who hire illegal immigrants.
2. Proposition 187 could end up costing taxpayers $ 10 billion.
3. Because Proposition 187 is poorly drafted, it directly conflicts with several important federal laws. As a result, California could lose billions in federal funding. Schools could lose more than $ 3 billion and Medi-Cal for senior and other legal residents could lose $ 7 billion.
4. It requires public school officials to thoroughly verify the citizenship of every child and every parent – more than 10 million people.
5. Proposition 187 would kick 400,000 kids out of school and onto the streets.
6. It threatens the health of all Californians because it would forbid doctors and nurses from giving immunizations or basic medical care to anyone suspected of being an illegal immigrant.
7. Every day, hundreds of thousands of undocumented workers handle the Californians' food supply in the fields and restaurants. Denying them basic health care would only spread communicable diseases throughout the communities and place every Californian citizen at risk.

Im Anschluss an die Diskussion kann der Inhalt des ersten Kapitels von *Part I* noch einmal kurz von den Schülerinnen und Schülern zusammengefasst werden. Diese Aufgabe hat wiederholenden Charakter, da dieses Kapitel bereits zusammengefasst wurde. Um einen Kontrast zur Auseinandersetzung mit der Einwandererproblematik auf einer rechtlichen und verallgemeinernden Ebene zu bilden, wird nun das Augenmerk auf die konkrete Gestalt des Delaney gerichtet. Man fährt mit der folgenden Fragestellung fort:

What conflict is there between Delaney's ideals and his behaviour after the accident? (Chapter I.1)

Delaney
- liberal-humanist ideals (p. 3)
- feeling of pity for the desperate situation of the Mexican (p. 9)
- environmentally-friendly person

versus

- does not call an ambulance, but offers money to the Mexican (p. 9)
- feeling of outrage against the Hispanics polluting the environment
- lies to the car dealer about the cause of the accident

Write a personal comment about the demands as stated in Proposition 187 on the basis of the discussion held in class.

Nachdem die Hausaufgabe kurz vorgetragen wurde, wird der Inhalt von Kapitel I.7, welches unter einem anderen Aspekt bereits bearbeitet wurde, kurz von einem Schüler oder einer Schülerin wiedergegeben. Dann werden die Schüler aufgefordert, in Gruppenarbeit den Konflikt zwischen Delaneys liberalem Humanismus und seinen konkreten Gefühlen Mexikanern gegenüber, wenn er tatsächlich mit ihnen konfrontiert ist, herauszuarbeiten. An konkreten Beispielen und Situationen sollen Delaneys Gedanken und sein Verhalten bei der Begegnung mit „illegalen" Mexikanern aufgezeigt werden, z. B. seine Überlegungen nach dem Diebstahl seines Wagens oder seine aufwallende Wut beim Anblick des Mülls um das Mexikanercamp herum.

Show the conflict between Delaney's ideal of liberal humanism and his feelings and thoughts when confronted with Mexicans. (Chapter I.7)

Es kann sich folgendes Tafelbild ergeben:

Delaney's ideal of liberal humanism
- tolerant position towards immigrants in the discussion with J. Jardine (p. 100f.)

versus

Delaney's feelings when encountering Mexicans
- Delaney feels anger and shame when meeting the Mexican again, but offers no help (p. 105)
- Delaney is led into thinking that Cándido threw himself deliberately in front of his car (p. 109)
- desire to destroy the Mexicans' camp because of litter (p. 112)
- encountering the two Mexicans Delaney wants them to be taken back to Mexico (littering the environment) (p. 117)
- Delaney imagines Cándido behind the driving wheel of his car after the theft (p. 120)

Das Unterrichtsgespräch wendet sich der Unterhaltung zwischen Delaney und J. Jardine Jr. in Kapitel I.3 zu. Als Einstieg dazu kann man den Abschnitt von Seite 46, Zeile 7 bis Seite 47, Ende vorlesen lassen. Daraufhin werden J. Jardine Jr.'s zentrale Äußerungen und Haltungen Mexikanern gegenüber herausgestellt. Des Weiteren sollte die Aufmerksamkeit der Schüler und Schülerinnen darauf gelenkt werden, dass die von J. Jardine Jr. verbreitete Stimmung als *foreshadowing* der im Folgenden geschilderten Plünderung des Camps angesehen werden kann. Hier kann auf unterstützenden Tafelanschrieb verzichtet werden. Als Hausaufgabe bietet sich an, dass sich die Lerngruppe mit der Widersprüchlichkeit Delaneys auf der Grundlage der im Unterricht erarbeiteten Ergebnisse noch einmal auseinander setzt.

Comment on the discrepancy between Delaney's ideals and his actual behaviour towards Mexicans.

Des Weiteren ist eine *summary* von Kapitel II.1 zu erstellen.
Zum ersten Teil der Hausaufgabe könnte sich z. B. folgende Ausarbeitung ergeben:

Delaney views Mexicans as types, not as individual human beings. The more contact he has with them, or the more he crosses their path in some way, the more dislike and aggression towards them wells up inside him. Although he does not insult or injure them deliberately, he feels a strong desire to have them removed from the country. His main concern is that the illegal immigrants produce a lot of litter that ruins the landscape.
Delaney is not aware of the discrepancy between his liberal ideals as voiced in his discussion with J. Jardine and his true emotions in actual encounters with Mexican people. An example of this can be seen in the fact that he tries to repress his feelings of guilt towards Cándido by telling himself that Cándido deliberately threw himself in front of his car.

Nach dem Vortragen des 1. Teils der Hausaufgabe (*comment*) werden die Schüler aufgefordert, sich zum Ausdruck *„a wound that refused to heal"* (p. 105) zu äußern. In diesem Unterrichtsgespräch wird der herausragende Aspekt des ersten Teils dieses *Component* noch einmal abschließend herauskristallisiert.

What does "a wound that refused to heal" mean? (Chapter I.7, p. 105)

Die Ergebnisse lassen sich kurz an der Tafel festhalten:

"A wound that refused to heal"

- since the accident Delaney has seemed to become more aware of the presence of Latin Americans in his "neighbourhood"
- despite the liberal-humanist label he cannot repress feelings of disgust

⇒ this conflict opens up a wound inside him

4.2 The long way to racism

Als Einstieg in den zweiten Teil des *Component* wird der zweite Teil der Hausaufgabe, die *summary* von Kapitel II.1, vorgelesen. Daraufhin wendet sich die Diskussion den beiden Mossbachers und den Situationen zu, in denen sie mit Mexikanern in Kontakt treten oder in denen ihre Aufmerksamkeit auf diese gerichtet wird. Die Schüler werden aufgefordert in arbeitsteiliger Gruppenarbeit die Situationen zu beschreiben, in denen Delaney und Kyra in Kontakt zu Mexikanern treten. Je eine Gruppe beschäftigt sich mit Delaney bzw. Kyra. Der Rahmen der gestellten Aufgabe würde den Umfang eines Tafelanschriebs sprengen, demzufolge werden die Ergebnisse anschließend mündlich vorgetragen. Um ein vollständiges Bild für jeden Schüler zu gewährleisten, wird jede Gruppe aufgefordert, sich die Ergebnisse der jeweils anderen Gruppe bei der Präsentation zu notieren.

How do the Mossbachers establish contact with Mexicans in Chapter II.1?

- the car dealer tells Delaney that rich Mexicans order their countrymen to steal cars in California (p. 145f.)
- Delaney hands his new car to the Hispanic parking valet and feels a moment of racist resentment (p. 149)
- the fear of another Mexican gang stealing his brand new car makes Delaney sit in the bushes watching his car instead of going on a hike (p. 155f.)
- Kyra becomes aware of how many Mexicans are hanging around Ventura Boulevard just a couple of blocks away from her business area and she decides to do something about it (p. 158f.)
- when Kyra buys something at a small supermarket she feels all the Mexican men's eyes on her; a young man offers himself as a cheap worker to her (p. 158f.)
- Kyra has decided to have a bigger fence because of what happened to Sacheverell; when she watches the Mexicans who work for her contractor she recognizes Cándido as the man who was hit by Delaney's car (p. 161)
- at the Da Ros' place Kyra notices a shopping cart in the brush; she checks the area and meets two trespassing Mexicans; she is afraid of them, but manages to make them leave (p. 161f.)

Als Hausaufgabe könnte man eine *creative-writing*-Aufgabe stellen, in der die Schüler und Schülerinnen aufgefordert werden, sich in die Person des Delaney, wie er in seiner Entwicklung bis zu Kapitel II.3 gezeigt wurde, hineinzuversetzen. Folgende Fragestellung ist denkbar:

Put yourself in the position of Delaney as he has been shown up to Chapter II.3 and describe the inner conflict between your humanist ideals and your actual feelings when encountering Mexicans.

Bei der Bearbeitung dieser Aufgabe sollten folgende Gedanken Delaneys, wie sie in Kapitel II.3 zum Ausdruck gebracht werden, erwähnt werden:

Delaney
- feels outnumbered by the Mexicans
  ("Mexicans", Delaney said, and there was no hesitation anymore [...], "there were Mexicans everywhere" (p. 184))
- still ponders on whether these people have the constitutional right to gather on a street corner (p. 185)
- wonders if you can assume people are illegal just because they are Mexicans (p. 185)

Der zweite Teil der Hausaufgabe besteht in der intensiven Vorbereitung von Kapitel II.5. Um den von Boyle suggerierten Vergleich zwischen *coyotes* und Mexikanern näher zu beleuchten, scheint es sinnvoll, zunächst einen Schüler ein Kurzreferat über *coyotes* halten zu lassen, in welchem neben der biologischen Beschreibung dieser Tiere auch arttypische Verhaltensweisen herausgestellt werden. Im Anschluss daran wendet sich das Unterrichtsgespräch Kapitel II.5 zu, in dem bestimmte typische Eigenschaften von *coyotes* erwähnt werden, die von den Schülerinnen und Schülern herausgearbeitet werden sollen. Des Weiteren sollte auf die Symbolik der *coyotes* im Hinblick auf Parallelen zum Verhalten der „illegalen“ Mexikaner eingegangen werden.

What are the characteristic features of coyotes as presented in Chapter II.5 and what symbolic meaning do they bear in relation to illegal Mexicans?

Characteristic features of coyotes:

- smart animals “Tricksters”
- coyotes manage to adapt to any new surroundings
- “coyotes keep coming, breeding up to fill in the gaps, moving in where the living is easy” (p. 215)
- “coyotes are cunning, versatile, hungry and unstoppable” (p. 215)

Symbolism

coyotes		**illegal Mexicans**
	– keep coming $\Rightarrow$ causes aggression	
- are fed		- are given jobs
	$\Rightarrow$ unnatural behaviour – are kept out by fences	
- around homes - kill pets		- along the border - steal food, invade
	$\Rightarrow$ results in fights over territory	

Der zweite Teil der Aufgabenstellung, die symbolische Komponente, kann auch als Hausaufgabe gegeben werden. Weiterhin sollte *Chapter* II.6 intensiv vorbereitet werden.

In der folgenden Stunde liegt der Schwerpunkt auf der Diskussion über Delaneys sich wandelnde Haltung zur Errichtung einer Mauer um das Wohngebiet bzw. zur wachsenden Zahl illegaler Immigranten, wie sie in *Chapter* II.6 gezeigt wird. Da drei Begegnungen von zentraler Bedeutung für die Fragestellung sind, bietet es sich an, in arbeitsteiliger Gruppenarbeit Delaneys Streitgespräch mit Kyra, seine Begegnung mit Todd Sweet und seine Begegnung mit dem Mexikaner hinsichtlich seiner Haltung Mexikanern gegenüber zu beleuchten.

Trace the development of Delaney’s position on the building of a wall and the presence of illegal immigrants. (Chapter II.6)

Da die Bearbeitung dieser Aufgabe zu recht ausführlichen Ergebnissen führt, wird auf einen Tafelanschrieb verzichtet. Die Ergebnisse der einzelnen Gruppen werden mündlich vorgetragen, wobei wiederum jede Gruppe aufgefordert ist, die Ergebnisse der jeweils anderen Gruppen zu notieren.

a) argument between Kyra and Delaney
Delaney
- resents being blocked out of nature (p. 220)
- disagrees with exclusion and division (p. 220)
- fears that being walled in will lead to bigotry (p. 224)

b) encounter with Todd Sweet
- Delaney agrees that the wall is offensive (p. 226)
- when asked for support Delaney suddenly
  - remembers all the unpleasant incidents involving Mexicans
  - feels his liberal attitude crumble
  - dreads fights with Kyra and Jack (p. 227)
- answers in an evasive way

c) encounter with the Mexican in his street
Delaney
- assumes that he is a trespasser (p. 229)
- approaches him in an aggressive manner
- is shocked about his own behaviour afterwards (p. 229)

Der zweite Teil der Stunde ist der Umsetzung der gefundenen Ergebnisse auf der stilistischen Ebene gewidmet. Dazu kann zur Wiederholung der Fachbegriffe noch einmal kurz *Worksheet 6* eingesetzt werden. Man kann damit fortfahren, den Abschnitt von S. 228, Z. 8 bis S. 229, Z. 21 vorlesen zu lassen. Im Unterrichtsgespräch werden die Stilmittel unter folgender Aufgabenstellung herausgearbeitet:

Identify the stylistic devices that Boyle uses to show Delaney's overreaction to the Mexican in his street. (Chapter II.6)

climax
- "the man looked startled, looked guilty – caught in the act" (p. 228)
- "this was the hiker, the illegal camper, [...] Delaney's life" (p. 228)
- "Delaney was nothing, a minor annoyance, [...] round his face" (p. 228)
- "the man was a thief, a liar, [...] a polluter, a Mexican" (p. 229)
  ⇒ Mexican as the highest gradation

parataxis
- "Delaney was hot. He was uncomfortable. He was aggravated." (p. 228)

Im Anschluss kann noch auf Todd Sweet als *telling name* eingegangen werden. *Sweet* kann im Zusammenhang des Romans so gedeutet werden, dass dieser Mann der wachsenden Zahl von Mexikanern freundlich und nicht aggressiv gegenübersteht. Er scheint der Einzige, der die Errichtung einer Mauer um das Wohngebiet ernsthaft verhindern will.

Als Hausaufgabe zur nächsten Stunde eignet sich die Zusammenfassung von Kapitel III.3.

Um den Schülern ein möglichst umfassendes Bild der Situation in Kapitel III.3 zu vermitteln, wird das Szenario am Anfang der Stunde um einige geographische Details erweitert, indem *Worksheet 8* bearbeitet wird.

Im ersten Teil sollten folgende Straßen und Gegenden herausgestellt werden: *Topanga State Park, Topanga Canyon, Topanga Canyon Boulevard, Ventura Boulevard, Sherman Way* und *Canoga Park.*
In der zweiten Aufgabe sollte auf die geographische Nähe zwischen der Wohnstätte der Mexikaner im *Topanga Canyon* und der *gated community* der Weißen hingewiesen werden. Obwohl beide so nahe beieinander liegen, gestalten sich die jeweiligen Wohnverhältnisse völlig konträr zueinander: luxuriöses, abgeschottetes Inseldasein auf der einen und kümmerliches Dahinvegetieren auf der anderen Seite. Beide Gebiete liegen nicht weit von Malibu entfernt, was zum gegenwärtigen Zeitpunkt als eines der attraktivsten und teuersten Wohngebiete Kaliforniens gilt.
Zudem ist durch die topographische Darstellung von *Sherman Way* und *Canoga Park* zu ermessen, wie lang und beschwerlich ein Fußweg vom Canyon dorthin für Cándido und América gewesen sein muss.

Notizen:

Worksheet 8

1. Identify the places mentioned in the book.
2. Comment on the contrast of the respective living areas.

In der folgenden Stunde wird anhand einer Textstelle Delaneys deutliche Wandlung zum Rassisten unter Betrachtung einiger möglicher Ursachen erarbeitet. Als Alternative zu diesem Vorgehen kann man diesen Themenkomplex aus dem Unterricht herausnehmen und ihn im Rahmen einer Klausur behandeln lassen (s. Klausuren, S. 12ff.).

Read excerpt p. 286, l. 12. until p. 290, l. 2. Find passages in this excerpt in which Delaney's racist behaviour comes to the surface. Give reasons for this change. (Chapter III.3)

Delaney's racist behaviour

Delaney

- is full of hatred on seeing the Latinos (p. 286)
- tells the police a lie (p. 287)
- attacks the Mexican without feeling guilt (p. 289)

Reasons

- accumulation of unfortunate occurrences related to Mexicans
  - car crashing into Cándido
  - theft of car
  - Kyra's fear on encountering the Latinos
  - fight over wall
- comsumption of alcohol
- Arroyo Blanco inhabitants turning into a mob
- raging fire
- deep fear of loss of possessions

⇒ attempt at finding a scapegoat

Eine geeignete Hausaufgabe zur nächsten Stunde besteht darin, Delaneys Verhaltensänderungen bei der Begegnung mit José und seinem Freund im Canyon, mit dem Zeitungsausträger und schließlich mit José und seinem Freund während des Feuers aufzuzeigen (Kapitel I.7, II.6, III.3).
In der folgenden Stunde wird eine abschließende Betrachtung der Person des Delaney hinsichtlich seiner vollkommenen Wandlung in einen blinden Rassisten aufgezeigt, der von der Vorstellung besessen ist, den illegalen mexikanischen Einwanderer Cándido unter allen Umständen zu stellen. Zunächst wird im Unterrichtsgespräch der Inhalt der Kapitel III.6, III.7 und III.8 skizziert. Alternativ können Zusammenfassungen zu den genannten Kapiteln von einzelnen Schülerinnen und Schülern im Rahmen einer Hausaufgabe angefertigt werden. Im nächsten Schritt werden die Kapitel III.6, 7, 8 unter folgender Fragestellung beleuchtet:

What are Delaney's ultimate steps and actions that show his complete transformation into a racist stalking Mexicans? (Chapter III.6/7/8)

Stalking the Mexicans

- exposing Cándido with the help of trip-wire cameras (p. 320)
- accosting Cándido on the road leading to the damage to Delaney's car (p. 333)
- acquisition of gun (p. 341)
- ignoring evidence presented by cameras (p. 346)
- finally tracking down the Mexicans in the shack (p. 351)

⇒ ultimate catastrophe

Es sollte an dieser Stelle noch auf einige symbolische Aspekte im letzten Kapitel eingegangen werden. Die Szene in der Hütte mit Cándido, América und dem Baby kann im biblischen Sinne als *Nativity Scene* angesehen werden, während die durch die schweren Regengüsse hervorgerufene *mudslide* zu einer Katastrophe führt, die man in einer ähnlichen Interpretation als *doomsday* ansehen kann.

Um die Lerngruppe abschließend zu einer kritischen Stellungnahme zum Roman bzw. zum Formulieren der persönlichen Eindrücke nach der Lektüre anzuregen, kann die folgende Rezension *Snobs and Wetbacks* aus dem *Time Magazine* vom 4.9.1995 vorgelegt werden. Alternativ kann man diese Rezension auch als Teil einer Klausur behandeln.

Notizen:

Snobs and Wetbacks – Sneering at the class divide

T. Coraghessan Boyle is an overpraised novelist with an unpleasant habit of sneering at his own cardboard characters. Some writers can carry this off, some can't. Aldous Huxley adopted a toplofty attitude toward his creatures, but he had the intellectual force to transform snobbery into satire. Among current 55 novelists, Martin Amis lacks intellectual force but is well supplied with nastiness, which occasionally resembles humor. Boyle merely sounds as if he needs an antacid.

His new novel, *The Tortilla Curtain* (Viking; 335 pages; $23.95) botches a good theme: the shuddering distaste of California's patio-living Anglos for Mexican illegals who perform the state's stoop labor. His pale hero is Delaney, a nature writer who has moved with his wife Kyra, a real estate shark, to a housing development above Topanga Canyon. Delaney is not just politically correct, he's politically exquisite, but when a Mexican man, Cándido, blunders in front of his white Acura on a canyon road, his reaction is angry revulsion: the wounded wetback, to whom he gives a $20 bill, is an infiltrator.

That's true. Cándido and his pregnant 17-year-old wife, decent folk down on their luck, huddle in a makeshift camp in the canyon and climb out every morning to find work at a labor exchange. But the sight of hungry Mexicans spooks Kyra's clients, and she sees to it that the exchange is shut. Delaney's liberal beliefs crumble, and he votes with other residents to build a wall, with a gate, around their development. The author, mistrusting his skill and the readers' acuteness, relentlessly flashes irony alerts. Cándido gets work constructing the wall, knowing well enough whom it is intended to keep out. Coyotes eat the nature writer's lapdogs, Osbert and Sacheverell. And when a mud slide sweeps Delaney toward mucky death, let there be no doubt whose brown, work-worn hand reaches to pull him free. This is weak, obvious stuff, worth a raised eyebrow and a shrug.

J.S.

Time Magazine, September 4, 1995

to sneer to express contempt by the expression on the face
toplofty supercilious

to botch to do sth badly or clumsily

stoop labor labor which can only be done with the body bent forwards and downwards

revulsion strong feeling of disgust
infiltrator sb who joins an organization secretly in order to spy on its activities

relentless never stopping or never becoming less intense

mud slide sth like an avalanche consisting of a wet, sticky mixture of earth and water
mucky very dirty
shrug raise of the shoulders to show that one is not interested in sth

Comment on this critic's words.

Die Bearbeitung dieser Aufgabe hängt stark vom persönlichen Leseeindruck des einzelnen Schülers oder der einzelnen Schülerin ab und lässt insofern keinen fest abgegrenzten Erwartungshorizont zu.
Man kann sich mit der Meinung des Kritikers einverstanden erklären und an Beispielen belegen, warum man die Protagonisten Delaney und Kyra für farblos gestaltet hält. Es lassen sich Belege dafür finden, dass Boyle sich im Roman an manchen Stellen über diese beiden Figuren regelrecht lustig macht, indem er einzelne Verhaltensweisen oder Charakterzüge überzeichnet, also eine ironische Distanz wahrt. Des Weiteren lassen sich konstruierte ironische Verflechtungen herausstellen, wie z. B. Cándido's Arbeit an einer Mauer, die gebaut wird, um Menschen wie seinesgleichen abzuhalten. Das Ende des Romans kann man als unglaubwürdig und unwahrscheinlich ansehen. Zum einen wird der Roman jäh und unerwartet beendet, zum anderen kann die Frage nach der literarischen Sinnhaftigkeit der Rettung Delaneys durch Cándido gestellt werden.
Auf der anderen Seite kann man eine andere Position als die des Kritikers einnehmen und herausstellen, dass die Figuren América und Cándido glaubwürdig und authentisch gestaltet sind. Es gelingt Boyle, ihre schwierigen Lebensumstände und die daraus resultierenden Versuche, aus einer verzweifelten Situation herauszukommen, plastisch und bewegend zu schildern. Es werden typisch lateinamerikanische Denkweisen an die Oberfläche gebracht, wie z. B. Cándidos innere Abneigung dagegen, dass er als Mann eine Zeit lang nicht für den Lebensunterhalt aufkommen kann. Der Autor beweist als Anglo-Amerikaner ein großes Einfühlungsvermögen in das Denken und Fühlen von Mexikanern.

Notizen:

Glossary of Spanish Words, Phrases and Sentences

a

¿Adónde vas, mi vida?	Where are you going, my love?
¿Alguién está aquí?	Is anybody here?
amigo	friend
A sus órdenes.	I'm at your service.
avenidas	avenues
¡Ay caray!	*exclamation:* Hell!

b

barrios	*here:* slums
basureros	people that live on the dump
bota	leather bottle
braceros	agricultural laborers
brinco	jumping
bruja	witch
Buenas.	*abbreviation:* Hi.
Buenas noches.	1. Good evening. 2. Good night.
Buenos días.	1. Good morning. 2. Good afternoon.
burrito	soft Mexican pancake with a filling of meat
burro	donkey

c

cabrón	husband who knows that his wife betrays him
caldo	soup
calles	streets
campesino	farmer
cándido	1. white. 2. innocent
cantina	saloon, pub
carnal	*informal:* buddy, friend
cementero	person that is addicted to sniffing cement
centavo	Mexican coin (cent)
cerros	hills
chicano	Mexican American
chiles	chilies
chingado	*Mexican slang:* bastard
chingón	*Mexican slang:* bastard, jerk
cholos	*offensive:* South or Central American Indian
chota	*Mexican slang:* police
ciento ochenta y dos	182
ciento ochenta y uno	181
cinco dólares	five dollars
cocido	stew
conquistadores	conquerors
Como hechas a mano.	Like hand-made.
compadre	*informal:* buddy, friend
compañero	comrade, friend
Comprendo.	I understand.
coyote	1. coyote. 2. refugee smuggler at the border between Mexico and the USA
criada	maid
curandera	witch doctor, Latin American medicine woman

d

dompe	*Spanglish:* dump

e

¿Eres sordo?	Are you deaf?
esquinas	street corners
Estados Unidos	United States

f

favelas	slums
fiesta	festivity, festival
flaco, -a	skinny, slim
frijoles	*Mexican:* beans

g

gabacho	*Mexican, offensive:* foreigner, especially (North) American
gastro	*abbreviation:* gastroenteritis
gatita	*affectionate:* little cat
giros	remittances
gringo	*offensive:* foreigner, especially (North) American
Gringolandia	*informal, offensive:* land of the foreigners
guantes	gloves
guatón	*informal:* fat man
güero	*Mexican:* blond

h

¿Habla usted español?	Do you speak Spanish?
hamburguesa	hamburger
hijo	son
hijo de la chingada	*Mexican slang:* son of a bitch
hombre	man
huaraches	*Mexican:* rustic sandals
huevos con chorizo	fried eggs with a spicy sausage
huevos hervidos con pan tostado	boiled eggs with toast
huevos rancheros	fried eggs with beans and tomatoes

i

indita	*affectionate:* little Indian
indocumentados	illegal immigrants

l

Laboratorio Médico	Medical Laboratory
ladrón	thief
latinos	people from Latin American countries
linda	pretty
Llame.	*here:* Name is.
loco	crazy
lucha	struggle

m

mala suerte	bad luck
'mano	*abbreviation:* brother, friend
manzanita	camomile
mapache	raccoon
marimba	instrument like a xylophone
Me llamo América	My name is América
mendigos	beggars
mercado	market
mi amor	my love
Migra	*abbreviation:* immigration officers, U.S. border patrol
mijo	*abbreviation:* my son
milagro de milagros	miracle of miracles
mi vida	*here:* my love
mojados	wetbacks; illegal immigrants
mole	dark Mexican sauce
momento	moment
muchacho	young man
Muchísimas gracias.	Thank you so much.
muy gacho	*Mexican slang:* very bad

n

nachos	hot corn chips with spicy melted cheese
niñitos	*affectionate:* little kids
niños	kids
No lo necesito.	I don't need him.
No problema.	No problem.
No quiero un matasanos.	I don't want a doctor.
el Norte	the North, the USA
norteamericanos	North Americans
novelas	novels

p

paisano	compatriot, fellow country-man
pandillero	gang member
papacito	daddy
Para las manos.	For the hands.
patrón	boss
pelirojo	red-haired
pendejo	*Mexican slang:* bastard, jerk
pinche	*Mexican slang:* fucking
pinche puta	fucking whore
poco	a little
Ponlos allá.	Put them over there.
pulque	alcoholic drink made of a-gaves

q

¿Qué onda?	*informal:* What's up? What's happening?
¿Qué pasa?	What's happening?
querido	honey; darling, love
¿Quieres joder conmigo?	*slang:* Do you want to fuck me?
¿Quieres trabajo?	Do you want to work?
Quiero trabajar.	I want to work.

r

ranchera	music typical of Northern Mexico
rebozo	shawl
reinas del cine	movie stars
rico	rich
romeritos	rosemary
rubio	blond
ruca	*Mexican slang:* sexy

s

sabe	know
salsa	sauce
señor	Mister
señora	Misses
señorita	Miss
serranos	spicy Mexican sausages
Si dios quiere.	If God wants it this way.
simpático	*here:* nice
socorro	help
sombreros	hats
supermercado	supermarket

t

taquería	snackbar that sells tacos (Mexican pancakes filled with meat, tomatoes, lettuce etc.)
tarjeta verde	Green Card
terminado	finished
tortilla	a round, thin Mexican pan-cake, usually eaten hot with a filling of meat etc.
trabaja	he (she) works
tragafuegos	firebreather
turistas	tourists

v

vago	bum, tramp
Vamos.	Let's go.
vías	small streets
vida	life
viejo	old
Virgen Sagrada	the holy Virgin

y

¿Y tú?	And you?
Yo soy.	I am.

Weiterführende Medien

Textsammlungen

- Augenbraun, H. und Stavans, I. (Hrsg.): Growing Up Latino. Reflections on Life in the United States. Boston, New York: Houghton Mifflin 1993
  Sammlung von Short Stories und Romanauszügen mit Einleitung und Literaturhinweisen
- Immigration. The U.S. Melting Pot Today. World and Press Special. Bremen: Eilers & Schünemann
  Zeitungsberichte mit Vokabelhilfen
- Kaiser, V. und Martin, J. (Hrsg.), Discover ... Hispanics in America. Paderborn: Schöningh 2002
- Kroner, B. und Simons, H. (Hrsg.): Materialienhandbuch Englisch. Band 3: Minorities. Köln: Aulis Verlag 1996
  Sammlung von fiktionalen und nicht-fiktionalen Texten mit Vokabelhilfen, Aufgabenstellungen, Lösungen, Wortfeldern
- USA Today. Dreams, Hopes and Disappointments. World and Press Special. Bremen: Eilers & Schünemann
  Zeitungsberichte mit Vokabelhilfen
- Tonn, H. (Hrsg.): Hispanic Groups in the USA. Berlin: Cornelsen 1994
- Trautmann, K. (Hrsg.): Hispanic Americans. Stuttgart: Klett 1989

Novels

- Alvarez, J.: How the García Girls Lost Their Accents. New York: Penguin Books USA 1992
  Der Roman beschreibt in 15 miteinander verbundenen Geschichten die interkulturellen Erfahrungen, die eine hispanische Immigrantenfamilie in New York macht.
- Cisneros, S.: The House on Mango Street. New York: Vintage Books 1984
  Der Roman erzählt in Form von Vignetten die Erlebnisse eines hispanischen Mädchens, das in Chicago aufwächst.

Short Stories

- Bradbury, R.: I See You Never. In: Tepe, Th. (Hrsg.): Twenty-one New Short Shorts. Stuttgart: Klett 1995, pp. 94-99
- Cisneros, S.: Geraldo No Last Name. In: The Before Columbus Fiction Anthology. Ed. by Ishmael Reed, Kathryn Trueblood and Shawn Wong. New York, London 1992, pp. 511f.
- Fondation, L.: Deportation at Breakfast. In: Tepe, Th. (Hrsg.): Twenty-One New Short Shorts. Stuttgart: Klett 1995, pp. 30-32

Poems

- Oliva, R.: The Immigrant Experience. In: Chicano Voices, ed. by Carlota Coridas de Burger. Boston, New York: Houghton Mifflin, pp. 80f.
- Soto, G.: Mexicans Begin Jogging. In: Los Angeles. Super City in the Golden State. Compiled and edited by Hanspeter Dörfel. München: Langenscheidt-Longman 1996, p. 21
- Piñero, Miguel: There Is Nothing New In New York. In: Schunk, Ferdinand (Hrsg.): New York Poems. Stuttgart: Reclam 1991

Songs

- Cruz, Celia: Latinos en Estados Unidos
- Ice-T: Born Dead, Virgin Records 1999, Album: Born Dead
- Molotov: Frijolero, Album: Dance and Dense Denso, 2002
- Springsteen, Bruce: The Line, Sony Music 1995, Album: The Ghost of Tom Joad

Zeitungsberichte

- Carlson, M.: Alienable Rights. In: TIME Domestic. 31.10.1994, Vol. 144, No. 18
- Dejesky, M.: Minorities use their poll power. In: The Independent 5.11.1998
- Foote, D.: Across the Borderline. In California, anger over immigrants is widening. In: Newsweek, 31.05.1993
- Gibbs, N.: Keep out, you tired, you poor ... Around the country, and especially in California, outrage over immigration is becoming electoral dynamite. In: TIME Domestic, 03.10.1994, Vol. 144, No. 14
- Gunson, Ph.: Migrants blocked from the US cities risk death in desert. In: The Guardian, 07.09.1998

- Gwynne, S.C.: The Unwelcome Mat. As the Proposition 187 debate roars, the U.S. begins an intensive effort to seal off a 2,000-mile border. In: TIME Domestic, 28.11.1994, Vol. 144, No. 22
- Reeves, Ph.: America slams its doors. In: The Independent, 16.02.95
- Tisdall, S.: Clinton proposes to block illegal aliens. In: The Guardian, 28.07.1993

Fernsehberichte
- „Flucht in die USA". Kabel 1: Die Reportage. Mai 1999, 55'
- „Kinder ohne Kindheit (4): Mexico – Notausgang ins Paradies". ZDF 12.08.1999, 45'
- „The Sound Of ... : Mexicans in California". Englisch Geographie bilingual. SWF, NDR, WDR, SF, DRS Schulfernsehen, 21.08.1998, 30'

Radiobericht
- „Nachts in dieser Kälte, auf dem Güterzug. Grenzgänger zwischen Mexiko und Nordamerika." WDR 1994
- „Die Illegalen. 3200 km entlang der Grenze USA/Mexiko." Feature von Friedrich Schütze-Quest. WDR 5 2006

Videomaterialien
- Immigration into the U.S.A.: The Mejias from El Salvador in Los Angeles (15')
  Entleihbar beim Institut für Film und Bild in Wissenschaft und Unterricht in den örtlichen Bildstellen.
- Minorities, Immigrants (1990, 30')
  Entleihbar über die USIS Video Library des Amerika-Hauses, Hardenbergstr. 22-24, 10623 Berlin.
- New Immigrants (1991, 15')
  Entleihbar über die USIS Video Library des Amerika-Hauses, Berlin.

Filme
- El Norte. Gregory Nava, USA 1983 *(drama)*
- Born in East LA. Cheech Marin, USA 1987 *(comedy)*
- My Family. Mi familia. Gregory Nava, USA 1995 *(drama)*
- Bread and Roses. Ken Loach, USA 2000 *(drama)*
- The Gatekeeper. John Carlos Frey, USA 2002 *(documentary)*
- Real Women Have Curves. Patricia Cardoso, USA 2002 *(comedy/drama)*
- A Day Without a Mexican. Sergio Arau, USA 2004 *(comedy, drama, fantasy)*
- Mojados – Through the Night. Tommy Lee Davis, USA 2004 *(documentary)*
- Spanglish. James Lee Brooks. USA 2004 *(comedy, romance, drama)*
- De Nadie. Tin Dirsamal, USA 2005 *(documentary)*
- La Migra. Juan Frausto, USA 2005 *(crime, drama, thriller)*

Internetadressen

Autor

http://www.tcboyle.com

http://www.tcboyle.de; webmaster@tcboyle.de *(deutschsprachige Website zu T.C. Boyle)*

Zeitungen

USA Today:	http://www.usatoday.com
New York Times:	http://www.nytimes.com
Los Angeles Times:	http://www.latimes.com
Washington Post:	http://www.washingtonpost.com
San Francisco Chronicle:	http://www.sfgate.com/chronicle
The Guardian:	http://www.guardian.co.uk
Hispanic Magazine:	http://www.hisp.com

Online-Nachrichten

http://www.pathfinder.com

http://pathfinder.com/time

http://www.cnn.com

http://www.newsweek.com *(Einige Artikel mit Unterrichtsvorschlägen)*

Landeskunde USA

http://www.usia.gov/uis.html	*(Homepage des United States Information Service)*
http://www.usbp.com	*(Website der Border Patrol, die sich als Organisation mit Informationen zu ihrer Geschichte, Aufgaben und Fotos vorstellt.)*
http://www.USBC.ORG/info/articles.htm	*(Zeitungsartikel, Essays, Leserbriefe zu verschiedenen Aspekten der Immigration)*
http://www.census.gov	*(Statistiken der Volkszählung zur Immigration)*
http://ca94.election.digital.com/e/prop/187/txt.html	*(Vollständiger Text der Proposition 187)*
http://ca94.election.digital.com/e/prop/187/for.html	*(Argumente für Proposition 187)*
http://ca94.election.digital.com/e/prop/187/against.html	*(Argumente gegen Proposition 187)*
http://home.att.net/~jackkurtz/tortcurt.html	*(Informationen und Fotos zur mexikanisch-amerikanischen Grenze)*
http://www.gegoux.com/topanga.htm	*(Gemälde des Topanga Canyon von Théodore Gégoux, 1850–1931)*
http://clnet.ucr.edu/murals/sparc/sparctour.html	*(Virtuelle Führung zu den ‚murals' von Los Angeles)*
http://www.altenforst.de/faecher/englisch/immi/index.htm	
http://www.langlong.de	*(Ideen- und Kopierecke des Langenscheidt-Verlages mit aktuellem Informationsmaterial zu den „Viewfinder Topics")*

Unterrichtsidee

http://www.englisch.schule.de/boyle/boyletop.htm	*(Unterrichtsvorschlag, Links zu weiteren Sachtexten, Schülerbeiträge, Fotos zu Boyles Roman „The Tortilla Curtain")*